HAKE'S
GUIDE TO
COMIC CHARACTER
COLLECTIBLES

AN ILLUSTRATED PRICE
GUIDE TO 100 YEARS
OF COMIC STRIP CHARACTERS

TED HAKE

WALLACE-HOMESTEAD BOOK COMPANY
RADNOR, PENNSYLVANIA

NOTICE

Values for items pictured in this book are based on the author's experience as well as actual prices realized for specific items sold through the catalogues of Hake's Americana & Collectibles mail and phone bid auctions. The prices are offered in this book for information purposes only. Many factors, including condition and rarity of the item, geographic location, and the knowledge and opinions of both buyers and sellers influence prices asked and prices paid. As the prices in this book are approximations, neither the author nor the publisher shall be held responsible for any losses that may occur through the use of this book in the purchase or sale of items.

CHARACTER COPYRIGHTS AND TRADEMARKS

For each illustrated item, and in the text of the book, we have acknowledged and identified the copyright holder and/or licensee wherever possible.

Items pictured (clockwise) in reduced form on the front cover are: Mickey Mouse celluloid toy, © Walt Disney Enterprises; Little Orphan Annie and Sandy dolls, © Harold Gray; Betty Boop book, © Max Fleischer; Popeye's Lucky Jeep toy, © 1929-36 King Features; Dick Tracy Target, © Famous Artists Syndicate, Inc.; Yellow Kid paper sign, © R. F. Outcault; Snoopy china bank, © 1966 United Feature Syndicate, Inc.; Buster Brown mug, © R. F. Outcault; Pogo ceramic figure, © 1959 Walt Kelly; Felix The Cat plate, © 1919, 1922, 1925 Pat Sullivan; Batman and Robin battery operated car, © 1972 National Periodical Publications, Inc.; Buck Rogers wind-up rocket, © John F. Dille, Co.; Hopalong Cassidy gun and holster set, © William Boyd; Howdy Doody wood figure, © Bob Smith; Roy Rogers lamp, © Roy Rogers. Item pictured on the back cover: Donald Duck teapot, © Walt Disney Enterprises.

We regret any omissions caused by error or the absence of identifying information on any item.

Copyright © 1993 by Ted Hake
All Rights Reserved
Published in Radnor, Pennsylvania 19089, by Wallace-Homestead,
a division of Chilton Book Company

No part of this book may be reproduced, transmitted, or stored in any form or by any means, electronic or mechanical, without prior written permission from the publisher.

Color photography by Mark Jenkins
Cover design by Anthony Jacobson

Library of Congress Cataloging-in-Publication Data
Hake, Ted.
    [Guide to comic character collectibles]
    Hake's guide to comic character collectibles : an illustrated
price guide to 100 years of comic strip characters / Ted Hake.
        p.   cm.
    Includes bibliographical references and index.
    ISBN 0-87069-646-7 (pbk.)
    1. Comic books, strips, etc.—Collectors and collecting.
I. Title.
PN6714.H35   1993
741.5′0973′075—dc20   92-50674
                                                             CIP

Manufactured in the United States of America

1 2 3 4 5 6 7 8 9 0   1 0 9 8 7 6 5 4 3

CONTENTS

COLOR PAGES

Big Little Books & Better Little Books
Dolls and Figures
Toothbrush Holders
Games
Tin Containers
Newspaper Comic Strip Promotional Buttons
Philadelphia "Evening Ledger Comics" Button Set
Newspaper Cowboy Comic Strip Promotional Buttons
Kellogg's Pep Cereal Button Set

ACKNOWLEDGMENTS

This book was prepared with assistance from my staff at Hake's Americana: Deak Stagemyer, Joan Carbaugh, Alex Winter and Vonnie Burkins. Special thanks are due Russ King and Jeff Robison for photography and research. My appreciation also goes to my wife, Jonell, and son, Ted, for their support, along with my thanks to the Wallace-Homestead staff for their contributions. Edward Kean and Jeff Judson kindly provided historical information about *Howdy Doody*.

USING THIS BOOK

Collectibles related to 75 comic strips or their individual characters are pictured, described and evaluated in this book. A total of over 1,500 collectibles are pictured with concentration on the earlier years of comic strip history but including examples from more recent times. Entries are organized as follows:

COMIC STRIP LISTINGS: The book is arranged alphabetically by the first letter of the strip's full title, disregarding the word ''THE'' when it is the first word of a title. Individual characters from a strip may be located by the book's index. Every attempt has been made to accurately identify individual strips by original creator(s) and newspaper syndicate when applicable.

COLLECTIBLES DATING: Each item description contains the actual copyright or syndication license date when so indicated on the item or its packaging. When dates are not available, a close assessment is made and indicated ''circa.''

COLLECTIBLES PICTURED: All collectibles in this book have appeared in mail and phone bid auction catalogs of Hake's Americana & Collectibles with the exception of some items currently in inventory for future auctions.

DESCRIPTIONS: Quotation marks indicate words actually appearing on the described item or its packaging. Information includes item size in decimal form rather than fraction form, e.g., 10.75″ to equal 10¾″, except fractions are used for sizes of pin-back buttons. The substance(s) used to produce the item are indicated, as is the item's manufacturer when known.

ABBREVIATIONS:

c.	= circa		
(D)	= Daily	(S)	= Sunday
bw	= black and white	br	= black and red
bwr	= black, white and red	rw	= red and white
bwbl	= black, white and blue	rwb	= red, white and blue

COMIC STRIPS: A BRIEF HISTORY

Forerunners of the comic strip dot the history of illustration. Examples begin with 12th century Japanese scroll art through the Middle Ages church gargoyles and into the 18th century satirical characterizations popular both in Europe and the United States. Scholars and historians have accurately documented many ''first'' or ''prototype'' examples in cartoons of both social commentary and an editorial or political nature that preceded the explosion of newspaper comic strips in major U.S. dailies at the outset of the 20th century. Among the most significant character styles were *Max and Moritz* by 1860s German creator Wilhelm Busch, obviously the basis of the later *Katzenjammer Kids*, and Palmer Cox's *The Brownies* beginning the 1870s.

For this book's purpose 1895 is chosen as a starting date. On May 5th of that year, the Sunday *New York World* first published a color panel titled *At the Circus in Hogan's Alley* created by Richard F. Outcault. The panel elaborately depicted an event in the lives of a group of slum urchins featuring a bald headed, buck-toothed waif in a nightshirt. The waif and his crowd quickly gained the attention of readers; the featured character became commonly known as ''Yellow Kid,'' due in most part to his recurring yellow nightshirt. His popularity was not lost on rival publishers. In a circulation war between Joseph Pulitzer's *World* and the *New York Journal* of William Randolph Hearst, Outcault's weekly Sunday panel moved to the *Journal* October 11, 1896, officially adopting the *Yellow Kid* title.

By late 1897, the *Journal* added *The Katzenjammer* Kids by Rudolph Dirks to its stable of fledgling cartoon or comic strip panels. The door was opened to an avalanche of immediately popular comic strips under various syndicates of the early 1900s.

Among the wealth of endearing and enduring strips begun in the 1900–1910 decade were *Foxy Grandpa, Happy Hooligan*, Outcault's new youngster *Buster Brown, The Newlyweds* (later to become *Bringing Up Father* featuring Maggie and Jiggs), the beautiful art noveau fantasy *Little Nemo in Slumberland, Mutt and Jeff* and *Toonerville Folks*.

Subsequent decades each added another notable list to comic strip lore and history. Among those surviving the longest and producing the most collectibles through the 1920s and beyond were *Barney Google, Little Orphan Annie* and *Moon Mullins*; 1929 was not a ''Depression'' year of new comic strip introduction. Two classic characters began their comic strip life: Tarzan, already a popular book character, and Popeye, already the star of the *Thimble Theatre* strip begun 10 years earlier. In addition, comic strips entered the space exploration and science-fiction age as Buck Rogers first awoke January 7, 1929, only to find himself already 500 years into the future.

The 1930s continued the proliferation of current and new comic strips. Among the new characters that remain popular to the present are Betty Boop, Blondie, Dick Tracy, Flash Gordon, Li'l Abner, Mickey Mouse and Snuffy Smith. Aviation and exotic settings became popular themes in the 1930s through such adventures as *Jack Armstrong, Smilin' Jack* and *Terry and the Pirates*. The late 1930s–early 1940s ushered in comic strip super heroes *Superman* and *Batman*, soon followed by a host of others.

World War II was the first war in U.S. comic strip history to generate lasting war-related strips. New heroes Don Winslow and Steve Canyon emerged, while a few standard characters such as Skeezix of *Gasoline Alley* went to war along with the readers. A cowboy named Red Ryder substantially had the western comic strip to himself through the 40s but found himself in a crowd from the beginning of the 1950s. Well-established western heroes Cisco Kid, Hopalong Cassidy, Gene Autry and Roy Rogers evolved into comic strips, partially due to revived popularity from the nation's new mass medium, television. Several new comic strips blossomed in the 1950s, notably *Pogo*, *Dennis the Menace* and *Peanuts*. In another 10 years, television's animated cartoon shows had displaced the printed comic strip as preferred entertainment and resulting collectibles. Many of the old standard strips, in the meantime, died off with their creators or by unsuccessful continuation by later artist(s) and/or writer(s).

Recent years have produced movie or TV revival versions of Buck Rogers, Superman, Batman, Li'l Abner, Orphan Annie and Dick Tracy for an entire new generation of collectibles. These and the few surviving comic strips of yesteryear plus some of the 1970s–1990s strip characters are already beginning to enchant collectors. But still unchallenged in popularity are the remaining collectibles from the superb early and growing years of comic strips and the hundreds of beloved characters they introduced to us.

TYPES OF COMIC STRIP COLLECTIBLES

Early collectibles were generally issued as retail merchandise items under copyright or license agreement by the strip's newspaper syndicate or, in some cases, only the strip's creator. Occasionally a collectible was offered either as a store or mail premium but this was not prevalent. Collectibles generally seem to have been produced with an eye toward youthful readers but certainly appeal of items to adults as consumers and parents was also considered.

Numerous variations of collectibles were conceived during a strip's lifetime. Actual comic strips are highly desirable, but rarely found in desirable or restorable condition. Original art is in strong demand, but examples are scarce, especially from the earliest years. Most popular among collectors are figurines or dolls in the image of the central character(s) of a given strip. Related toys are also very desirable, and demand remains consistently high for early picture pin-back buttons.

Illustrated storybooks were a mainstay item for all major strips. Several printed popular strips in a single volume and, during the 1930s–1940s, Whitman Publishing Co.'s ''Big Little Books'' or ''Better Little Books'' were published in large quantities. Several comic strips or characters from them were featured on product advertising cards, and these are sought equally by comic and advertising collectors.

Other popular comic collectibles include signs and posters, games, paint or printing sets, pencil boxes, jigsaw puzzles, chinaware, glassware, handkerchiefs or other fabrics, toothbrush holders, pencil holders, banks, candy containers, planters, salt and pepper sets, simulated jewelry, lamps. This listing is certainly not inclusive but represents the most frequently produced items.

Most collectors eventually specialize in mementos from their preferred strip(s). Others will specialize in a particular type of collectible, e.g., games, regardless of a particular strip origin.

CONDITION

As with any collectible, the better the condition the better the value. Collectors can reasonably expect that items will have been used, particularly if from the earlier years. Most collectors will accept normal minor wear on an item if otherwise in complete condition. Obvious heavy wear, defacement, permanent soiling, and missing parts or accessories all quickly reduce the value of an item. Original packaging, if it was provided, is equally important to most collectors since packaging, especially for early era items, seldom remains and is found only rarely on items in optimum condition. Packaging was used mostly for larger toys, dolls or similar large items and occasionally may have newspaper syndicate copyright date, name of maker and other information that may not appear on the item itself. The value of a mail premium is enhanced greatly if the original mailing container and enclosure leaflets are intact. Repair or cleaning may increase an item's value if done with care, caution and expertise. Crude repairs or harsh cleaning can just as easily decrease normal value.

The following terms and definitions are used to describe items in Hake's Americana & Collectibles auctions. These definitions are fairly standard throughout the collectibles hobby, although some dealers, who do not describe each item in detail, have adopted a shorthand system wherein the letter "C" for "Condition" and a number from 1 to 10 is used to designate condition. In this system "C10" equals "mint," "C9" equals "near mint" and so on. The system used at Hake's Americana is:

Mint: Flawless condition. Usually applied to items made of metal or items that are boxed or otherwise packaged. MIB stands for "Mint in box."

Near Mint (NM): Just the slightest detectable wear but appearance is still like new.

Excellent (Exc.): Only the slightest detectable wear, if any at all. Usually applied to buttons, paper and other non-metallic items. Also used for metallic items that just miss the near mint or mint level.

Very Fine (VF): Bright clean condition. An item that has seen little use and was well cared for with only very minor wear or aging.

Fine: An item in nice condition with some general wear but no serious defects.

Very Good (VG): Shows use but no serious defect and still nice for display. Metal items may have detail or paint wear. Paper items may have some small tears or creases.

Good: May have some obvious overall wear and/or some specific defect but still with some collectible value.

Fair: Obvious damage to some extent.

Poor: Extensive damage or wear.

At Hake's we grade our items conservatively; less than 1% of the 20,000 items we sell annually are returned due to an error in describing the item's condition. However, in the collectibles business much wishful thinking occurs regarding condition, particularly by less experienced dealers and among the general public attempting to sell items found around the house. When purchasing items through the mail, it is best to have a clear understanding with the seller that the item can be returned for a refund if the item has more wear or damage than the seller specified.

PRICES

Comic strip collectibles have been a staple of Hake's auctions beginning with the first catalogs in the late 1960s. Prices realized have increased steadily for those items obtained and auctioned at moderate intervals. No meaningful means of price comparison is available for an extremely rare or "one of a kind" item if offered only once, or at most twice but in different condition, over a 25-year period.

Several factors determine the value of a comic strip collectible. The price estimates in this book assume excellent, complete condition without damage or any significant wear. These prices are based on the author's experience, auction prices realized, sales lists and typical show prices. There are no absolutely correct prices regarding collectibles. Supply and demand, along with the buyer's satisfaction are the final criteria influenced by:

1.   CONDITION—wear and damage obviously detract from an item's value. Many price guides admonish collectors to accept only "mint" items and the resulting competition for the relatively few items that truly meet this criteria results in premium prices for "mint" items. Original boxes, particularly for toys, can often add 50% or more over the price for a comparable unboxed example. The collector who can emotionally live with less than "mint" items has a powerful bargaining chip and can often acquire items that are visually perfect for a fraction of the cost for items truly "mint."

2.   COMPLETENESS—this factor applies to items with several to many parts or accessories. Typical items are games and figures. If the item was played with, there is a good chance small pieces were lost. In the absence of a box or instruction sheet, it is difficult to determine if in fact the item is complete so it is best to have an understanding with the seller if the item is being sold as complete or as is. Figures, particularly painted figures such as a bisque, may have paint loss ranging from minimal to extensive and distracting. Figures or dolls of fragile substances such as bisque, celluloid or composition may have missing fingers or toes to the detriment of price.

3.   DESIGN FEATURES—aesthetics play a role in determining value. Items made with quality materials, excellent graphics, or some special unique feature will set themselves apart from similar but less appealing objects and command a higher price.

4.   CROSSOVER INTEREST—quite a few items appeal to more than one group of collectors. For example, a Buster Brown game could be of intense interest to game collectors, Buster Brown collectors, and very possibly shoewear collectors. Each type of collector probably has his or her own opinion of the item's value, but this sort of multiple interest can create higher asking prices and/or spirited auction bidding.

5.   RARITY—competition for rare items related to popular strips or characters stimulates high prices, but rarity alone does not force prices up. There are many rare items available at reasonable prices for those strips not among the ranks of the most popular. Likewise, if little merchandise was produced for a strip, the item may be exceedingly rare but not sought after because there is not enough variety to inspire the attempt to build a collection.

6. DISTRIBUTION—obviously early comic strip collectibles were distributed more heavily in northeastern and midwestern states. While it's reasonable to assume that many items have now proliferated throughout the country by regional shows, move of owner, etc., prices generally tend to be higher on the east and west coasts. Along with denser populations, these areas have larger concentrations of collectors looking for similar items.

7. EMOTIONS—both dealers and collectors of comic strip collectibles have a fond appreciation for the objects, which accounts for the excitement and satisfaction derived from the quest to obtain them. These emotions also come into play in the pricing of items and the decision whether or not to make a purchase. Balancing the factors just discussed, as well as becoming aware of the state of the market through show attendance, review of sales list prices and auction results and communication with other collectors and dealers, will all contribute to making the correct decision when faced with the crucial question—should I or shouldn't I pay this much?

REPRODUCTIONS AND FANTASY ITEMS

Reproductions and fantasy items rarely occur in comic strip collectibles and, except for several crossover interest examples of western hero collectibles, normally are not a serious problem for collectors.

Reproductions are items made as similar as possible to an original item, unfortunately with the probable intent of defrauding the buyer. Fantasy items are those never licensed and not even existing during the time period of the original collectibles. They are, in short, conceived and produced well after the fact.

Specific reproduction examples are tin signs for Kayo Chocolate Drink, Howdy Doody Twin Pops, and Bond Bread signs of both the Lone Ranger and Hopalong Cassidy. Reproduction or fantasy pin-back buttons exist for several comic characters and cowboy personalities, usually detectable by poorer printing quality or modern plastic coverings.

Reproduction attempts are most frequent, at this time, for western hero collectibles. Blatant examples are the Lone Ranger Silvercup Bread membership pin, a Roy Rogers/Trigger six-point brass star badge and a Hopalong Cassidy six-point silver star badge. Many of these reproductions are detectable by an oval plate on the reverse with two raised areas to anchor the bottom bar of the pin.

Western hero fantasy items include 1 inch diameter lightweight plastic pencil sharpeners that have a screened image of Roy Rogers or Hopalong Cassidy; these individuals have also been pictured on a fantasy yellow fabric scarf with heavy black ink portrait images. Recently licensed western items include two sets of western character knives. Camillus Cutlery issued 11 different in their *Riders of the Silver Screen* series (4.75″ long) and Barlow issued five different in their *Sunset* series (3.5″ long). Both sets feature character illustrations in full color under clear acrylic handles.

Collectors can quickly gain a sense of fraudulent or fantasy items through communication with reputable collectible dealers as well as fellow collectors with similar interests. Purchases always preferably should be made from a known source who guarantees authenticity, completeness and condition.

COLLECTING TIPS

Comic strip collectibles are not abundant, particularly those of earlier years. Examples will generally appear at most good-sized antiques shows or flea markets, at advertising and paper memorabilia shows, and occasionally at general antiques shops or cooperative antiques stores. Garage sales and yard sales are generally not a likely source of collectibles of any significant vintage or condition, although such sources should not be disregarded out of hand. Relatives and friends should not be overlooked, and some collectors try classified ads in local newspapers. In addition to the enjoyment of personal searching, collectors also have the option of bidding in auctions, such as those of Hake's Americana, where merchandise is pre-selected on the basis of popular demand.

A beginning collector may well be satisfied acquiring any type of item that suits the fancy and budget. Eventually most collectors elect to specialize to some degree rather than build a random collection from the many different options in comic strip character collecting. Options include concentrating on a single comic strip or character(s) from it or on comic memorabilia from different strips but by the same single creator such as Richard Outcault, George McManus or Milton Caniff. Many collectors prefer to specialize in similar items from any comic strip, e.g., figurines and/or dolls, paper items, games, pin-back buttons; or by substance, e.g., celluloid, metal, bisque.

Once a collection starts to grow, three factors become important considerations: care, storage and security. An essential aspect of collecting is preservation. Collectibles are tangible artifacts of our history and, hopefully, every collector wishes to pass on collected objects without having them damaged while acting as caretaker. This seems so basic, and yet there are people who will use pencil or even ink to write a price or other notes on a paper item or book cover. Adhesive stickers are often applied to fragile fabric and paper items. Finally, there are those devoted to repairing tears with copious amounts of tape. These are not proper conservation methods. Prices or notes can be made on separate papers, stickers placed on Mylar sleeves rather than on the item, and nonstaining archival paper tape can be used on damaged paper. Repairs or cleaning should always be done judiciously.

Restoration or touching up of original surfaces on dimensional items may be necessary for desired display appearance. Professional restoration is, of course, preferable. Otherwise skill and caution are advised. A repainted bisque figure gains no value by garish or improper use of color and/or crude application. Glued repairs should be done as inconspicuously as possible. Critical restorations on delicate substances such as composition or celluloid should be left to an individual familiar with these substances if the particular item has significant enjoyment or monetary value to the owner. Toy mechanism repairs or replacements are also generally better done professionally if, for no other reason, the repair person's access to repair parts which are likely obsolete.

Other perils to collections include dust, smoke, moisture and sunlight. Glass cases for three-dimensional items can overcome the dangers of soiling and yellowing from dust and smoke. The same is true for glass framing of paper items. Drapes can block bright sunlight to eliminate fading. In most environments, housing a collection in the living area will be enough to avoid the dangers of excessive heat, cold, moisture and silverfish found in attics and basements.

Glass frames, known as Riker mounts, work well for the flat storage of celluloid button collections; however, if the lining in the bottom tray is cotton, in high humidity areas the cotton will attract moisture that will extensively damage the backs of buttons before any signs of damage appear on the front. Litho buttons may adhere to the glass and lose paint when removed. Many button collectors also use plastic sheets with pockets designed to hold coins. This works provided litho buttons are not placed in the sheets. Some sheets contain chemicals that react with the inks on the buttons to virtually melt the ink after a period of time. If these sheets are used at all, they should be stored vertically rather than flat to keep the accumulated weight off the bottom sheets.

The best place for storing both celluloid and litho buttons and other small items is in a cabinet with stacks of shallow drawers. Such cabinets are available (they are also favored by coin collectors). The cabinet provides darkness and protection from dust and smoke, there is no pressure on the objects, and the doors can be locked for security.

Proper security is always a matter of personal judgment. To some, the prevailing security of the dwelling itself is adequate. Others may opt for the security of safety deposit boxes offered by banks, although this obviously hinders casual enjoyment. Some insurance companies offer specialized policies against theft or other loss, although most will require a detailed inventory listing and/or a professional appraisal of monetary value before underwriting a collectibles policy.

Whatever collecting preference is established, comic strip collectibles are available in many price ranges and delightful options. This book is designed as an overview and guide to this fascinating collecting field.

Alphonse and Gaston

Creator: Frederick B. Opper.

Began: Sundays, 1902. Hearst Syndicate.

Principal Characters: Alphonse, Gaston, Leon.

Synopsis: Humor strip featuring the excessive politeness and deferral to each other by Alphonse and Gaston, inevitably to the detriment of both and often their Parisian friend Leon. The characters originally were blended into other early strips by Opper, including Happy Hooligan, And Her Name Was Maud.

1

2

1
POSTCARD 3.5x5.5″ full color card cut from sheet issued by American Journal Examiner © 1906. $15

2
POSTCARD 3.5x5.5″ bw c. 1906. $12

3
MECHANICAL POSTCARD 3.5x5.5″ © 1906 American Journal Examiner. $15

3

4

4
CLAY PIPE 5″ long terra cotta with painted figures of them and lady above inscription on stem "After You Dear Gaston." German made c. 1906. $50

5
HANDKERCHIEF 12x12″ bwr six-panel comic strip cloth with Opper copyright c. 1906. Photo example shows entire handkerchief and detail of the last panel. $35

6
HANDKERCHIEF 12x12″ bwr six-panel comic strip cloth with Opper copyright c. 1906. Photo example shows entire handkerchief with detail of last panel. $35

6

5

The Amazing Spider-Man

Creator: Stan Lee (writer), Steve Ditko (artist)

Began: Amazing Fantasy (Marvel Comics #15, Aug. 1962); as newspaper strip 1979.

Later Artists and/or Writers: John Romita, Roy Thomas, Gerry Conway, Gil Kane, Ross Andru, Jim Mooney, Artie Simik, others.

Principal Characters: Spider-Man (alter ego Peter Parker), Aunt May, recurring villains including Lizard, Green Goblin, Kraven the Hunter.

Synopsis: Spider-Man is an acrobatic crimefighter distinguished by the strength, wiles and capabilities of an actual spider. The popularity of the character has also extended into animated and live TV series, paperbacks, and merchandise items.

1
BUTTON 3.5″ full color in 4x7″ retail pack. From 1966 copyright "Super Hero Club" series. $20

2
HAND PUPPET 11″ vinyl in 9.5x16″ retail pack. By Ideal Toy Corp. © 1966 Marvel Comics Group. $100

3
"SKY DIVING PARACHUTIST" 4.5″ plastic figure in 7.5x11″ retail pack. By Azrak-Hamway © 1973 Marvel Comics Group. $35

1 **2** **3**

4
BOARD GAME in 9.5x19″ box including playing board also picturing Incredible Hulk, Sub-Mariner, Iron Man, Mighty Thor. By Milton Bradley © 1967. $20

4

5
ACTION FIGURE 8″ jointed hard plastic in 7x10″ retail pack. By Mego Toys © 1979 with card text in French for Canadian or overseas market. $30

6
"ENERGIZED SPIDER-MAN" 12″ battery operated action figure in 9x13.5″ retail box. By Remco Toys © either 1978 or 1979. $50

7
"MARVEL COMICS SUPER HEROES" embossed steel lunch box with plastic bottle issued as set by Aladdin Industries © 1976. BOX $20, BOTTLE $10

8
FRICTION TOY 2x3x4″ long lithographed tin vehicle with soft vinyl Spider-Man head. By Marx Toys © 1968. $125

5 **6**

7 **8**

Barney Google

Creator: Billy DeBeck

Began: (D) 6/17/19. Hearst Syndicate.

Later Artists and/or Writers: Fred Lasswell.

Principal Characters: Barney Google, his horse Spark Plug, black jockey Sunshine.

Synopsis: Immensely popular humor strip that transpired from early *Married Life* strip by DeBeck in which Barney was first known as "Aleck." The Google name came in 1919, and in 1922 his lovable but pathetic race horse Spark Plug was introduced. DeBeck added Snuffy Smith into the strip in 1934. After about five years the strip was retitled to include both names. Snuffy gradually replaced Barney as the central character.

1

2

3

4

5

6

1
BARNEY GOOGLE/SNUFFY SMITH 8.5x10.75" original inked and pencilled comic art by Billy DeBeck signed and dated by him in 1935. $700

2
"BOSTON SUNDAY ADVERTISER" 11x17" cardboard colorful sign promoting Sunday comics readership c. 1930s. $200

3
BARNEY GOOGLE 5x18" original bw ink and pencil accent art by Billy DeBeck scheduled for publication September 28, 1931. $400

4
"BARNEY GOOGLE AND SPARK PLUG GAME" in 9x17" box. Game art is by Billy DeBeck and game pieces include stand-up figures and playing board, all shown in our photo with box lid. By Milton Bradley Co. © 1923. $200

5
"SPARK PLUG" .25x4x5" long wooden toy on wheels. DeBeck signature and both 1922, 1928 copyright. $150

6
"SPARK PLUG" 8x9" long wooden pull toy in three hinged sections. DeBeck signature c. late 1920s-1930s. $200

7
"SPARK PLUG" 1.5x3x4" long rubber squeaker toy © 1923. $150

8
"SPARK PLUG" 1.5x3x4" long clear glass candy container with tinted accent paint © 1923. $75

9
SHEET MUSIC 9x12" c. 1930s. $40

10
"MUSICAL ALBUM" 9.25x12" song folio with 16 pages including other non-related song hits © 1923. $50

11
SUNSHINE 4x8.5x9.5" tall painted wood pull toy with cast iron front wheels. Patent date October 26, 1926. $200

12
JOINTED WOOD DOLL 8.5" tall with fabric outfit. By Schoenhut Toys c. 1920s. $500

13
PAINTED BISQUE FIGURE 9" tall c. 1930s. $75

14
STUFFED CLOTH DOLL 12" tall c. 1930s. $150

15
"BARNEY GOOGLE" 4.5x6" book by Saalfield Publishing Co. © 1935. $75

16
"COMIC MONTHLY" 8.5x9" newsstand comic Vol. 1 #11 from 1922 with 28 pages. $75

17
BARNEY GOOGLE ON SPARK PLUG 2.5x3" tall painted lead paperweight c. 1930s. $150

18
BARNEY GOOGLE & SNUFFY SMITH 3" tall painted plaster salt and pepper set depicting them in military outfits c. 1940s. SET $40

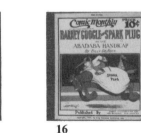
7

8

9

10

11

12

13

14

15

16

17

18

Batman

Creator: Bob Kane

Began: 5/39. Detective Comics; newspaper syndication 1943 and 1966.
National Periodical Publications.

Later Artists and/or Writers: Numerous

Principal Characters: Batman (alter ego Bruce Wayne), Robin the Boy Wonder (alter ego Dick Grayson originally), Joker, Riddler, Penguin, Catwoman.

Synopsis: Enduring "Dynamic Duo" crimefighting team that achieved greatest popularity by comic books, movie serials, TV series of 1966, full-length movie of 1989. The latter two each resulted in hundreds of merchandise items. A *Batman Returns* spinoff movie was released in 1992.

1
"BATMAN" 7″ tall ceramic bank
© 1966 N.P.P. $55

2
"ROBIN" 7″ tall ceramic bank
© 1966 N.P.P. $55

3
BATMAN "CAPTAIN ACTION" uniform and equipment for 12″ Captain Action doll in 11x15x2.5″ deep box © 1966 Ideal Toy Corp. $300

4
BATMAN 27″ tall cloth doll with vinyl face. Photo example is missing cape. c. 1966. $100

5
BATMAN 14″ tall cloth doll with vinyl face and fabric cape.
c. 1966. $75

6
BATMAN 10″ tall "Soaky" plastic soap bottle © 1966 N.P.P. $75

7
ROBIN 10″ tall "Soaky" plastic soap bottle © 1966 N.P.P. $75

8
BATMAN 4″ tall "Pez" candy plastic dispenser of earliest version with removable cape. c. 1966.   BLUE CAPE AND HOOD $80, IF BLACK $250

9
"ROBIN" 8″ tall clothed plastic action figure on 7x10″ card © 1977 Mego Corp. $60

10
"BATGIRL" 7.5″ tall clothed plastic action figure on 7x10″ card © 1977 Mego Corp. $150

11
"BATMAN" 6x8.5" bw paper mask with reverse side introduction for daily and Sunday comic strips. c. 1943. $175

12
BATMAN & ROBIN 7x10.5" tall paper mask with full color Batman image on one side and Robin on the other. © 1966 N.P.P., offered as "General Electric Television" premium. $15

13
BATMOBILE 3.5" tall by 4.5" wide by 12" long metal and plastic battery operated Japanese toy © 1972 N.P.P. $100

14
"TALKING BATMOBILE" 3" tall by 4" wide by 9" long battery operated plastic toy in 3.5x4.5x10" box by Palitoy of England © 1977. $200

15
"BATMAN" 8.5" tall hard vinyl bank © 1974 Mego Corp. $50

16
"JOKER" 8" tall hard vinyl bank © 1974 Mego Corp. $60

17
BATMAN 12" tall plastic helmet disguise by Ideal Toy Corp. © 1966 N.P.P. $75

18
"BATMAN" fabric costume and plastic mask in 3.5x11x13" tall box © 1966 Ben Cooper Co. $45

19
"BATMAN" 3" tall painted metal figure pin in 3.5x5" retail pack © 1966. $40

20
ROBIN 3" painted figure pin in matching 3.5x5" retail pack to #19. © 1966. $40

11

12

13

14

15

16

17

18

19

20

21

22

23

24

25

26

27

28

29

30

31

32

21
"MY BATMAN COLLECTION"
pair of 5.5x8.5″ plastic holders, each
with inset 10 numbered metal coins
forming complete set of 20 coins.
© 1966 N.P.P.   SET $125, EACH
COIN $4

22
"CHARTER MEMBER/BATMAN &
ROBIN SOCIETY" 3.5″ full color
celluloid button © 1966. $12

23
"BATMAN & ROBIN DEPUTY
CRIME FIGHTER" 3.5″ full color
celluloid button © 1966. $35

24
BATMAN "TALKING ALARM"
2.5x6.5x7″ tall plastic clock
© 1974.   TALKING $100, NOT
TALKING $50

25
"BATMAN" plastic figure assembly
model kit in 2.5x7x13″ tall box
© 1964 Aurora Plastics Corp. $200

26
"ROBIN" plastic figure assembly
model kit in 2x5x13″ tall box © 1966
Aurora Plastics Corp. $100

27
"BATPLANE" plastic assembly
model kit in 1.5x5.5x13″ wide box
© 1966 Aurora Plastics Corp. $250

28
BATMAN & ROBIN 16x20″ full
color paper picture c. 1966. $45

29
BATMAN & ROBIN pair of matched
27x40″ full color paper posters
© 1966 N.P.P.   EACH $35

30
"BATMAN MAKES A MIGHTY
LEAP INTO NATIONAL POPULAR-
ITY" March 11, 1966 issue of Life
magazine with cover article. $12

31
BATMAN & ROBIN 3.5x5.5″ full
color photo fan card c. 1966. $15

32
"BATMAN" 11x13.5″ "Paint By
Number Book" © 1966 Whitman
Publishing Co. $30

33
"BATMAN ROAD RACING SET"
featuring 3.5″ long Batmobile and
Joker cars, racing channel tracks, battery equipment in 2x11x13.5″ wide
box. © 1976. $300

34
"BATMAN MAGIC-MAGNETIC
GOTHAM CITY" three-dimensional
cardboard and plastic playset by
Remco Industries in 4x18x24″ wide
box. © 1966 N.P.P. $600

35
"BATMAN JIGSAW PUZZLE
GAME" set in 3.5x7x8″ wide box.
By Milton Bradley Co. c. 1966. $35

36
"BATMAN GAME" by Milton Bradley Co. in 2x9x18″ wide box.
© 1966. $35

37
"BATMAN CARD GAME" by Ideal
Toy Corp. in 1.5x6.5x10″ wide box.
c. 1966. $35

38
"BATMAN AND ROBIN"
6.75x8x3.75″ deep embossed steel
lunch box c. 1966 by Aladdin Industries.   BOX $125, BOTTLE $60

39
"BATMAN CHUTE" 4.5″ tall plastic
figure with vinyl parachute on 8.5x11″
card © 1966. $35

40
"BATMAN AND ROBIN THE BOY
WONDER" 5″ tall white plastic "Sip-
A-Drink" cup. © 1966. $35

41
BATMAN 3″ tall white glass mug
with portrait in black. Reverse has
different illustration. c. 1966. $15

42
"BATMOBILE" 4x7.25″ embossed
metal license plate © 1966. $30

43
"BATMAN" 4.5x10″ vinyl fold-out
school supply kit that opens to 10x12″
with interior full front view of Batman. c. 1966. $50

44
"BATMAN/ROBIN" 9.5″ tall litho-
graphed metal oval waste can © 1966
N.P.P. $75

33

34

35

36

37

38

39

40

41

42

43

44

Beetle Bailey

Creator: Mort Walker

Began: (D) 9/4/50; (S) 9/14/52. King Features Syndicate.

Principal Characters: Beetle Bailey, Sgt. Snorkel, Otto (Snorkel's dog), Lt. Fuzz, Lt. Flap, Chaplain Staneglass, Zero, Plato, Killer Diller, Gen. Halftrack, Miss Buxley.

Synopsis: Humor strip about the misunderstandings and misadventures of military training life at Camp Swampy. Beetle was first introduced as a college student whose Army enlistment in 1951 began his career as the perpetual trainee.

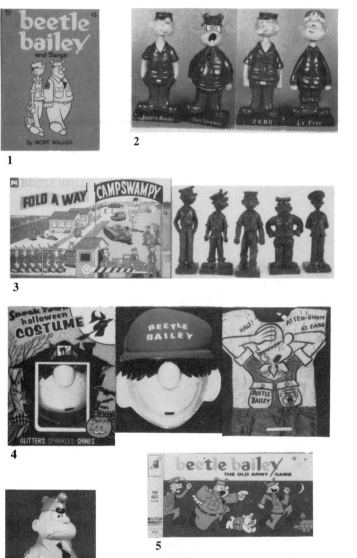

1
"BEETLE BAILEY AND SARGE" 6.5x9″ first printing edition book with 64 pages by Dell Publishing Co. © 1958. $20

2
BEETLE BAILEY & FRIENDS 7.5″ tall painted composition bobbing head figures c. 1960s.   EACH $75

3
"BEETLE BAILEY FOLD-A-WAY CAMP SWAMPY" plastic and paper playset featuring character figures about 2.75″ tall. Set is in 2.5x12x20″ wide box. © 1964 Multiple Products. $175

4
BEETLE BAILEY "SPOOK TOWN HALLOWEEN COSTUME" of full-length fabric outfit and thin plastic face mask in 3x8.5x11″ tall box c. 1960s. $40

5
"BEETLE BAILEY/THE OLD ARMY GAME" in 2x9.5x19″ wide box. © 1963 Milton Bradley Co. $30

6
SGT. SNORKEL 11″ tall painted composition figure bank c. 1960s. $75

7
BEETLE BAILEY 5x5x8″ wide ceramic mug sized to serve equally well as a planter. c. 1960s. $50

Believe It Or Not!

Creator: Robert L. Ripley

Began: 1919. New York Globe.

Later Artists and/or Writers: Paul Frehm, Walter Frehm.

Synopsis: The outgrowth of a sports oddity feature by Ripley, expanded to a daily single panel illustrating bizarre, incredible or unbelievable curiosities based on fact. Ripley claimed documentation for each item, and the strip was occasionally imitated by others throughout its lengthy publication life.

1

"PAIN PROOF MAN" 21x27.5"
bwbl poster c. 1930s. $100

2

"BELIEVE IT OR NOT!" Whitman
Big Little Book #760 © 1931. $50

3

"BELIEVE IT OR NOT!" 6x9" book
© 1929. $25

4

"BELIEVE IT OR NOT!" 2.5x3"
cards published as set of 48 in
1937. CARDS 1-24 EACH $7,
CARDS 25-48 EACH $25

5

"BELIEVE IT OR NOT!" 5x6" New
Year's 1940 card folder.
© 1940. $25

6

"BELIEVE IT OR NOT!" 4x9" cardboard ink blotter © 1937. $8

7

"BELIEVE IT OR NOT!" 4x9" cardboard ink blotter © 1937. $8

8

"BELIEVE IT OR NOT!" 4x9" cardboard ink blotter © 1937. $8

9

"BELIEVE IT OR NOT!" set of
seven handkerchiefs in 7x9" box c.
1930s. SET $80, EACH $10

10

"BELIEVE IT OR NOT!" 2.5x3.5"
Fleer Gum wrapper © 1970.
WRAPPER $8, CARD SET $40

Betty Boop

Creator: Max Fleischer

Began: (D) 7/23/34; (S) 1935. King Features Syndicate.

Principal Characters: Betty Boop, her pet dog Bimbo, clown friend Koko.

Synopsis: Strip featuring the animated cartoon vamp character created originally in 1931 by Fleischer. Her characteristics from the outset included a huge head with spitcurls, enormous large eyes, small shapely body, a thigh garter, small heart symbol on her outfit. Her appeal prompted countless merchandise items in the 1930s, as well as various print or film revivals into the 1990s.

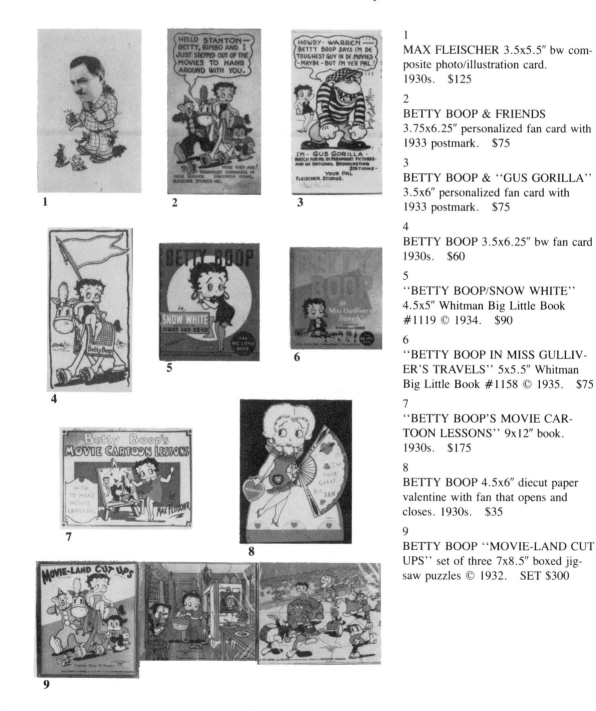

1
MAX FLEISCHER 3.5x5.5″ bw composite photo/illustration card.
1930s. $125

2
BETTY BOOP & FRIENDS
3.75x6.25″ personalized fan card with 1933 postmark. $75

3
BETTY BOOP & ''GUS GORILLA''
3.5x6″ personalized fan card with 1933 postmark. $75

4
BETTY BOOP 3.5x6.25″ bw fan card 1930s. $60

5
''BETTY BOOP/SNOW WHITE''
4.5x5″ Whitman Big Little Book #1119 © 1934. $90

6
''BETTY BOOP IN MISS GULLIVER'S TRAVELS'' 5x5.5″ Whitman Big Little Book #1158 © 1935. $75

7
''BETTY BOOP'S MOVIE CARTOON LESSONS'' 9x12″ book.
1930s. $175

8
BETTY BOOP 4.5x6″ diecut paper valentine with fan that opens and closes. 1930s. $35

9
BETTY BOOP ''MOVIE-LAND CUT UPS'' set of three 7x8.5″ boxed jigsaw puzzles © 1932.   SET $300

10
"BETTY'S ACROBAT" 10″ tall trapeze toy in 1.5x6x9″ box.
1930s. $2500

11
"BETTY BOOP" 7″ tall celluloid wind-up toy in 3x3x7.5″ tall box. 1930s. $500

12
"BETTY BOOP HULA DANCER" 8″ tall wind-up 2.25x3x8″ tall box.
1930s. $700

13
HELEN KANE 9x12″ blw/orange sheet music with cover photo of her, known as the Boop-Oop-A-Doop singer who sparked the creation of Betty Boop. © 1929. $25

14
"BETTY BOOP" 21″ tall wood guitar. 1930s. $250

15
BETTY BOOP 12″ tall jointed wood and composition doll. 1930s. $750

16
BETTY BOOP 6″ tall painted bisque figure with movable arms.
1930s. $1000

17
BETTY BOOP 3.75″ tall painted bisque figure. 1930s. $90

18
BETTY BOOP 2.75″ tall painted bisque figure. 1930s. $90

19
BETTY BOOP 14″ tall painted composition figure. 1930s. $300

20
BETTY BOOP 14″ tall painted composition figure © 1931. $300

21
BETTY BOOP 15″ tall painted plaster carnival statue. 1930s. $150

10

11

12

13

14

15

16

17

18

19

20

21

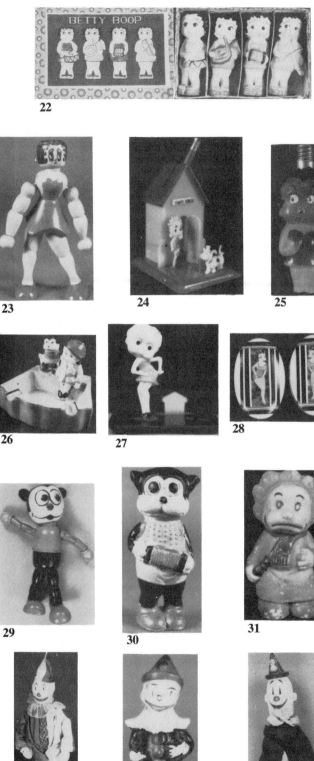

22

23

24   **25**

26   **27**

28

29

30   **31**

32   **33**   **34**

22
BETTY BOOP set of four 3.25″ tall painted bisque figures in 5.5″ wide box.   BOXED $450, EACH $75

23
BETTY BOOP 4.5″ tall painted and jointed wood doll © 1931. $150

24
BETTY BOOP ''HAPPY HOUSE'' 2x2.5x2.5″ tall celluloid pencil holder c. late 1940s. $1200

25
BETTY BOOP 3″ tall frosted glass bulb. 1930s. $40

26
BETTY BOOP/BIMBO 3.5x4x3″ tall china ashtray. 1930s. $150

27
BETTY BOOP 1.75″ tall painted celluloid figurine c. 1930s. $150

28
BETTY BOOP pair of convex celluloid ovals 1.5″ wide by 2.25″ tall for decoration on horse bridle. 1930s.   PAIR $150

29
BIMBO 7.5″ tall jointed and painted wood figure. 1930s. $300

30
BIMBO 3.5″ tall painted bisque figure. 1930s. $50

31
BILLY BOOP 2.5″ tall painted bisque figure. 1930s. $100

32
KOKO 10″ tall jointed wood doll in fabric outfit. 1930s. $400

33
KOKO 2.75″ tall painted bisque figure. 1930s. $50

34
KOKO 11″ tall fabric hand puppet with vinyl head © 1962 Gund Co. $75

35
BETTY BOOP/BIMBO 5.5″ tall china wall sconce with convex front and flat plane back. 1930s. $175

36
BETTY BOOP 12x15″ stuffed fabric toy quilt with thickness of about 1″. 1930s. $100

37
BETTY BOOP 16″ tall stuffed cloth doll in 3x9x19″ tall box. c. 1970s or later. $35

38
BETTY BOOP/BIMBO enameled metal double pin on 2.5x3″ sales card. 1930s.   ON CARD $150, LOOSE $100

39
BETTY BOOP/BIMBO gold colored metal double pin on 2.25x3″ sales card. 1930s.   ON CARD $150, LOOSE $75

40
BETTY BOOP 2″ diameter silvered brass pocketwatch. Back has engraved portrait of her and Bimbo. 1930s. $750

41
BETTY BOOP 1 ⅛″ full color lithographed metal pin-back button.   1930s. $40

42
″BETTY BOOP CO-ED″ deck of bridge playing cards in 2.5x3.75″ box. 1932. $75

43
″BETTY BOOP AND BIMBO″ bridge card double deck with score pad in 3.5x4.5″ box. 1935. $200

44
BETTY BOOP 4.5″ tall metal animated alarm clock in 3x5.25x6″ tall box. Animated part is Bimbo's head that rocks back and forth. © 1983. $100

35

36

37

38

39

40

41

42

43

44

Blondie

Creator: Chic Young

Began: September 1930. King Features Syndicate.

Later Artists and/or Writers: Dean Young, Jim Raymond, Michael Gersher, Stan Drake.

Principal Characters: The Bumstead Family—Blondie, Dagwood, Baby Dumpling (early), Cookie, Alexander, Daisy and her pups, Mr. Dithers and wife Cora, Herb and Tootsie Woodley, Mr. Beasley (mailman).

Synopsis: One of the most consistent high-circulation strips featuring the harried, hectic daily and Sunday adventures of the Bumsteads. The strip inspired nearly 30 movies between the late 1930s and early 1950s plus two later television series.

1
CHIC YOUNG 3.5x5.5″ signed bw greeting card. 1967. $75

2
CHIC YOUNG 4.5x5.5″ signed bw greeting card. 1967. $100

3
''BLONDIE & DAGWOOD'' 5x7.5″ storybook with 92 pages. Example photo shows front cover and title page. © 1936. $35

4
BLONDIE 6x7″ book by McKay Co. © 1944. $25

5
''BLONDIE/COOKIE AND DAISY'S PUPS'' Whitman Better Little Book #1491 © 1943. $30

6
BLONDIE 8x11″ Whitman Co. paint book © 1944. $20

7
BLONDIE 8.5x11″ Whitman Co. coloring book © 1950. $20

8
''BLONDIE IN THE MOVIES'' 10.5x14.25″ paperdoll book by Whitman Co. © 1941. $200

9
''BLONDIE CUT-OUT DOLLS'' 10.5x13″ Whitman book © 1941. $200

10
BUMSTEAD FAMILY steel toy baby stroller 12x15x17″ tall by Nassau Products. © 1949. $100

11
"DAGWOOD'S SANDWICH"
4.5x5.5" Christmas card for 1939 by
Hallmark. $15

12
"DAGWOOD'S SOLO FLIGHT" tin
wind-up toy 9" long with 11.5" wing
span. © 1941 by Marx Toys. $350

13
"PENNY SINGLETON-ARTHUR
LAKE" 8x10" Dixie Ice Cream pre-
mium picture. Back has scenes from
undated but 1941 movie "Blondie
Goes Latin." $15

14
"DAGWOOD" 5" tall composition
wood figure © 1944. $60

15
"ALEXANDER" 3.5" tall composition wood figure. © 1944. $75

16
"COOKIE" 2.75" tall composition
wood figure. © 1944. $75

17
"DAISY" 4x12x12" tall soft rubber
squeaker toy. 1940s. $150

18
"BLONDIE PLAYING CARD
GAME" by Whitman 5x6.5" box
© 1941. $30

19
"BLONDIE GOES TO LEISURE-
LAND" premium game by Westing-
house Electric Co. in 8x11" envelope
© 1940. $30

20
"BLONDIE AND DAGWOOD'S
RACE FOR THE OFFICE GAME"
7x10" box. c. 1950. $30

21
"BLONDIE PAINTS" 1x4.5x5.5"
wide tin watercolor kit © 1948. $25

22
BLONDIE 7x8.5x4" deep flat steel
lunch box and 6.5" metal thermos.
© 1969 set by King-Seeley Co.
BOX $75, BOTTLE $30

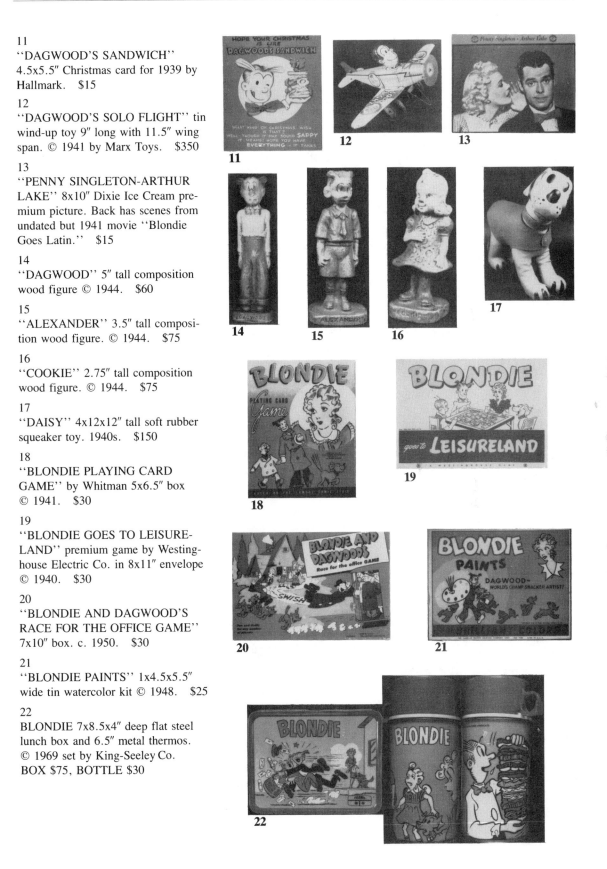

Bonzo

Creator: George E. Studdy

Began: 1930-1931. King Features Syndicate.

Principal Characters: Bonzo

Synopsis: A very popular puppy dog character of the 1920s-1930s in both United States and Europe. Bonzo, a spotted white pup, usually smiling and often accented by a wink expression, accounted for numerous merchandise items even before news syndication.

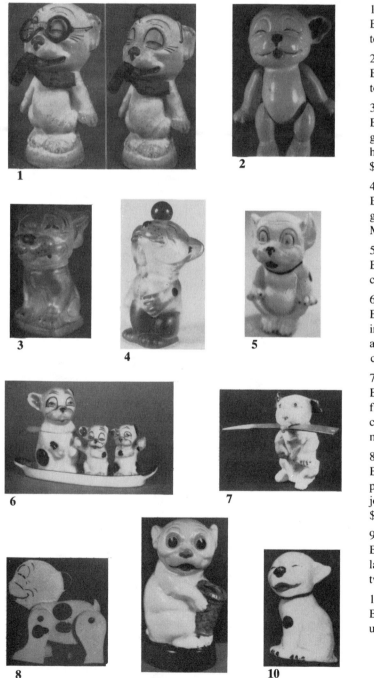

1
BONZO 6.5″ tall painted hollow plaster bank. 1928. $75

2
BONZO 4″ tall jointed celluloid figure toy c. 1930s. $150

3
BONZO 3″ tall frosted clear camphor glass perfume bottle with removable head. English copyright c. 1930s. $45

4
BONZO 3″ tall transparent camphor glass perfume bottle by Potter & Moore of England c. 1930s. $35

5
BONZO 4.5″ tall painted bisque figure c. 1930s. $50

6
BONZO china condiment set consisting of 3″ tall sauce holder, smaller salt and pepper shakers, platform tray. c. 1930s. $100

7
BONZO 3.75″ tall painted white metal figure with slotted mouth that holds celluloid letter opener. Made in Germany c. 1930s. $60

8
BONZO 1.5x4x4.5″ tall jigsawed and painted commercial wood toy with jointed legs, head and tail c. 1930s. $75

9
BONZO 3x3.5x5.5″ tall china figure lamp base with bulb holder held between the paws. 1930s. $200

10
BONZO 2.75″ tall white bisque figure. 1930s. $50

11

BONZO set of four 3″ tall painted bisque figures, each depicted playing different musical instrument.
1930s.   EACH $25

12

BONZO 7″ diameter china dish German made c. 1930s. $20

13

BONZO 2.25″ diameter palm puzzle c. 1930s. $40

14

"COWAN'S BONZO TOFFEE"
1x1.75x2.75″ tall lithographed tin candy container c. 1930s. $100

15

BONZO 6″ diameter silvered metal trivet on 3″ metal legs. 1930s. $75

16

"BONZO'S ANNUAL" 7.5x10″ book published by Dean of England with 124 pages © 1951. $35

17

"BONZO'S ANNUAL" 7.5x10″ book published by Dean of England with 94 pages c. early 1950s. $35

18

"TRICKY BONZO" 6x7″ storybook with 40 pages by McLoughlin Bros. © 1929. $35

19

"BONZO-A DOG'S LIFE" 5x8″ pencil tablet. c. 1930s. $25

20

BONZO 3.5x5.5″ British postcard by Valentine. c. 1930s. $15

21

BONZO 3.5x5.5″ British postcard by Valentine c. 1930s. $15

22

BONZO 3.5x5.5″ British postcard by Valentine c. 1930s. $15

23

BONZO 3.5x5.5″ British postcard by Valentine c. 1930s. $15

24

BONZO 3.5x5.5″ British postcard by Valentine c. 1930s. $15

11

12

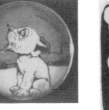

13

14

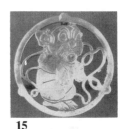

15

16

17

18

19

20

21

22

23

24

Bringing Up Father

Creator: George McManus

Began: (D) 1/12/13; (S) 4/4/18. Hearst Syndicate.

Later Artists and/or Writers: Zeke Zekely, Vernon Greene, Frank Fletcher, Hal Camp, Frank Johnson, Warren Sattler, Bill Kavanaugh, Hal Campagna.

Principal Characters: Jiggs, Maggie, daughter Nora, tavern owner Dinty Moore.

Synopsis: The culmination of several earlier strips by McManus, and one of only a few strips to gain international familiarity. The recurring theme of Jiggs' escapes from domination by Maggie to visit Dinty Moore's saloon remained popular through two generations of readers.

1

2

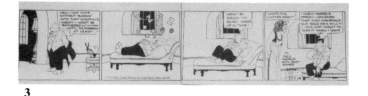

3

4

5

6

7

8

1
"JIGGS AND I" 10.5x13.5" issue of Collier's magazine for Jan. 19, 1952 with George McManus article. $15

2
JIGGS 7x11" cardboard display sign for Sunday comic section of Boston Advertiser c. 1930s or earlier. $75

3
BRINING UP FATHER 5.25x21.75" stiff white paper with original art inked in black by McManus for daily newspaper strip scheduled for publication June 14, 1932. Last panel has an added personal greeting from McManus to recipient. $150

4
JIGGS 32" tall probably home made and painted wood figure with full color Jiggs portrait likeness on each side. Possibly intended as umbrella holder. c. 1930s. $300

5
JIGGS 7.5" tall doll by Schoenhut Toys with painted composition body parts, jointed metal ball bearing arms and legs, stuffed cloth torso.
c. 1920s. $400

6
JIGGS 11" tall painted plaster figure c. 1920s. $75

7
JIGGS, MAGGIE, NORA set of 9" tall painted plaster figurines
c. 1920s.   EACH $60

8
JIGGS 5" tall jointed and painted wood doll with his name stamped on chest. c. 1930s. $125

9
"BRINGING UP FATHER" set of 4"
tall painted bisque figures in
1x4.25x5" wide box © 1934.
BOXED SET $300, EACH $50

10
"JIGGS" 4.25" tall composition wood
figure © 1944. $60

11
"MAGGIE" 5" tall composition wood
figure © 1944. $60

12
JIGGS & MAGGIE 2.75" tall plastic
figures c. 1950s. EACH $15

13
JIGGS 5" tall red clay planter
c. 1930s. $25

14
JIGGS & MAGGIE 2.5" tall china salt
and pepper set with china holder tray
c. 1930s. $100

15
"BRINGING UP FATHER IN SOCI-
ETY" 10x13.5" songbook
© 1915. $25

16
JIGGS 6.5" wide tin lunch box c.
1930s. $100

17
"BRINGING UP FATHER" 10x10"
book by Cupples & Leon Co.
© 1919. $30

18
"BRINGING UP FATHER" 10x10"
book by Cupples & Leon Co.
© 1927. $30

19
"BRINGING UP FATHER/THE BIG
BOOK" 10x10" book by Cupples &
Leon Co. © 1926. $75

20
"BRINGING UP FATHER" Whitman Big Little Book #1133
© 1936. $30

21
"BRINGING UP FATHER"
8.5x11.5" Whitman paint book #663
© 1942. $35

9

10 **11** **12**

13 **14** **15**

16 **17** **18**

19 **20** **21**

The Brownies

Creator: Palmer Cox

Began: Circa 1880s by various publications.

Synopsis: Although not a comic strip in the traditional sense, The Brownies cartoons are considered a forerunner of character style to blossom in the early 1900s. The host of unnamed and mute wee folk created by Cox resulted in numerous merchandise items, probably the earliest character series to do so.

1
PALMER COX AUTOGRAPH
3.5x4.5″ white card signed in ink
''Palmer Cox, Brownieland, March
17th, 1906.'' $100

2
BROWNIE 4″ tall full color china
planter c. 1890s. $100

3
BROWNIE 6″ tall full color china humidor or cigar holder. The lid cap in photo example is possibly a replacement. Word ''Defender'' is on the cap brim molded as part of the head.
c. 1890s. $150

4
BROWNIE POLICEMAN 7.5″ tall
full color china figure with small
depression at top of hat, probably intended to hold a candle.
c. 1890s. $150

5
BROWNIE SAILOR 9″ composition
figure in painted blw outfit.
c. 1890s. $75

6
BROWNIES 5″ tall full color stuffed
cloth dolls c. 1890s.   EACH $75

7
BROWNIE 3″ tall cast iron figure
with original brown paint.
c. 1890s. $90

8
BROWNIE 5″ long painted cast iron
toy depicting Brownie in driver's seat
of a racing sulky. Paint finish is silver
with red wheels. c. 1890s. $275

9
BROWNIE 7″ tall wood figure toy
with jointed arms and legs.
c. 1890s. $20

10
BROWNIES 3.25″ tall colorful white china mug. 1890s. $100

11
BROWNIES 2.5″ tall colorful white china cup. 1890s. $35

12
BROWNIES 3.5″ tall white china toy teapot with color art of Brownies playing instruments. 1890s. $75

13
BROWNIES 2″ tall white china cup with full color art of Brownies playing baseball. 1890s. $40

14
"BROWNIE YEAR BOOK" 10x12.5″ hard cover picturing monthly Brownie activities. Published by Mc-Loughlin Bros. © 1895. $125

15
"BROWNIE FAMILY DECALCOM-ANIE ALBUM" 2.5x4.25″ booklet of decals. 1890s. $25

16
BROWNIE 4x4.5″ full color diecut stand-up from series of 1890s premiums by Lion Coffee. $15

17
"MERRY CHRISTMAS FROM THE BROWNIES" 2x3x4.5″ wide yellow cardboard candy box. 1890s. $65

18
"BROWNIE CAMERA" 4x4x6″ wide box holding Eastman Kodak Co. snapshot camera. Late 1890s. $150

19
BROWNIE 6.5″ brass charm bracelet suspending three 1″ tall Brownie charms plus two replica rifle charms. c. 1898. $40

20
"BABY BROWNIES" 1x7.5x9.5″ wide box containing set of 12 wood blocks by Superior Type Co. c. 1910. $75

10   11   12

13

14

15   16

17   18

19   20

Buck Rogers in the 25th Century

Creator: Phil Nowlan (writer), Dick Calkins (artist)

Began: (D) 1/7/29; (S) 1930. John F. Dille Co. Syndicate.

Later Artists and/or Writers: Many

Principal Characters: Buck Rogers, his girlfriend Wilma Deering, Dr. Huer, Killer Kane, Ardala Valmar, Black Barney.

Synopsis: The classic science-fiction strip, known equally for its futuristic adventures and prophetic examples of space hardware. The strip spun off into a 1930s radio series, 1939 and 1979 movies, a brief 1950-51 television series, and a 1979-81 TV series. The original comic strip ceased in the mid-1960s and revived in 1979 into 1983.

1
"AMAZING STORIES" 8.5x11" magazine for Aug. 1928 with first Buck Rogers story "Armeggedon-2419 A.D." $200

2
BUCK ROGERS 12x18" newspaper comic strip premium portrait c. 1932. $500

3
"MAP OF THE SOLAR SYSTEM" 18.5x25.5" full color paper premium by Cocomalt c. 1933-1935. $500

4
"BUCK ROGERS SOLAR SCOUTS" 5x8" manual for "Secret Club Of The Radio Friends Of Buck And Wilma" Cream of Wheat premium of 1936. $175

5
"BUCK ROGERS SOLAR SCOUTS" 1.5" tall brass badge Cream of Wheat premium for 1936. $50

6
"BUCK ROGERS SOLAR SCOUTS" 1.75" tall badge for "Spaceship Commander" Cream of Wheat premium for 1936. $150

7
"BUCK ROGERS" paper Helmet and Rocket Pistol in envelope. Cocomalt premium c. 1933-1935 available in version for either Buck Rogers or Wilma. EACH SET $300

8
"BUCK ROGERS SOLAR SCOUTS" Repeller Ray Ring Cream of Wheat premium for 1936. $600

9
BUCK ROGERS 6x8″ Kellogg's booklet. 1932-1933. $125

10
"STRANGE ADVENTURES IN THE SPIDER SHIP" 8x9″ Blue Ribbon Press pop-up book. $250

11
"BUCK ROGERS PAINT BOOK" 11x14″ Whitman © 1935. $100

12
BUCK & WILMA 7.5x10″ Cocomalt picture 1933-1935. $100

13
TOOTSIETOY 4.75″ "Destroyer" spaceship in box. 1939. $250

14
TOOTSIETOY 4.75″ "Attack Ship" metal spaceship in box. 1939. $250

15
TOOTSIETOY 4.75″ "Battle Cruiser" metal spaceship in box. 1939. $250

16
BUCK ROGERS 1.75″ tall Tootsietoy metal figure. 1939. $100

17
WILMA 1.75″ tall Tootsietoy metal figure. 1939. $100

18
"BUCK ROGERS ROCKET RANGERS" 2.25x4″ membership card. c. 1935. $150

19
"BATTLE FLEET" 10.5x16.5″ illustration sheet of rocketship balsa wood models. c. 1934. $175

20
BUCK ROGERS 2.25x3″ card #446 from © 1936 set of 24 strip cards #425-448.   EACH $40

21
BUCK ROGERS 12″ long tin wind-up rocketship by Marx Toys, 1934. $500

22
BUCK ROGERS 12″ long wind-up rocketship by Marx c. 1935. $600

9

10

11

12

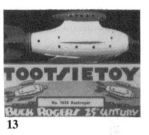
13

14

15

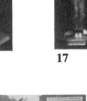
16

17

18

19

20

21

22

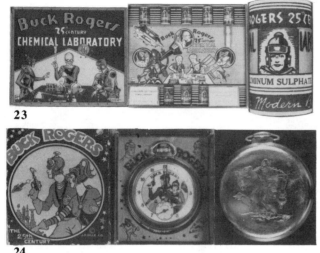

23

24

25 **26**

27

28

29

30 **31** **32**

23
"CHEMICAL LABORATORY"
chemistry kit in 1.5x11.5x13.5" wide
box. © 1937. $400

24
BUCK ROGERS pocketwatch in
2.5x2.5" box with insert card. Case
back has engraved space monster.
1935. BOXED $750, WATCH
ONLY $400

25
BUCK ROGERS 9.5" long blued
metal Rocket Pistol XZ-31, first issue
by Daisy in 1934. $125

26
BUCK ROGERS 7.5" long blued
metal Rocket Pistol XZ-35, second
smaller version by Daisy Mfg. Co.
c. 1935. $100

27
BUCK ROGERS 9.5" long Atomic
Pistol version of 1936 by Daisy Mfg.
Co. with copper finish. $300

28
BUCK ROGERS 7" long red and yel-
low Liquid Helium Water Pistol by
Daisy Mfg. Co. c. 1936. $300

29
"U-238 ATOMIC PISTOL AND
HOLSTER SET" of 10.5" long pistol
plus leather holster in 2x6x9.5" wide
box. 1948 version by Daisy Mfg. Co.
that also issued 1946 version titled
Atomic Pistol U-235. PISTOL $200,
HOLSTER $150, BOX $150

30
"BUCK ROGERS" 2.5x3" story
booklet published by Whitman in
1935 obtained for 12 Tarzan Ice
Cream cup lids. $150

31
"THE ADVENTURES OF BUCK
ROGERS" 7.5x9.5" Whitman Big
Big Book © 1934. $100

32
"BUCK ROGERS 25TH CENTURY
A.D." Whitman Big Little Book
#742 © 1933. $50

33
BUCK ROGERS 2.25" brown/white
Dixie lid c. 1936. $35

34
BUCK ROGERS 8x10" Dixie picture
c. 1936. $90

35
BUCK ROGERS & WILMA 15x18"
paper sign. © 1940. $250

36
''CRAYON SHIP'' 2x5" wide box
that exposes a planetary view as box
is opened and closed. Example photo
shows front and back panel.
1930s. $75

37
''ASTRAL HEROES PRINTING
SET'' in 1x6.5x9" wide box by
StamperKraft c. mid-1930s. $300

38
''COSMIC CONQUESTS PRINTING
SET'' in 1x10x12" wide box by
StamperKraft c. mid-1930s. $300

39
''ROCKET RANGERS'' 1.5" wide
rwb lithographed tin tab c. late
1940s. $35

40
''SATELLITE PIONEERS'' 2" diameter bwr lithographed tin tab c. late
1940s. $35

41
''SPACE RANGER KIT'' of punch-
outs by Sylvania TV c. 1952 in
11x15" envelope.   UNUSED $125

42
BUCK ROGERS GAME by Transogram c. late 1950s in 2x10x18" wide
box. $60

43
''SONIC RAY'' 9" plastic flashlight
pistol with code folder in 2x8x10"
wide box c. early 1950s.   BOXED
$150, GUN ONLY $75

33

34

35

36

37

38

39

40

41

42

43

Bugs Bunny

Creator: Warner Brothers Studios, producer Leon Schlesinger

Began: (S) 1/10/43. Newspaper Enterprise Association. (D) mid-1940s.

Later Artists and/or Writers: Many contributors.

Principal Characters: Bugs Bunny, inept rivals Elmer Fudd and Yosemite Sam, various Warner Brothers sidekicks.

Synopsis: This internationally-known, wise-cracking rabbit first emerged in late 1930s animated cartoons; his comic book debut was in 1941 in the first issue of Looney Tunes & Merrie Melodies. His unwavering jaunty attitude and catch-phrase ''What's Up Doc?'' have propelled him to immense popularity and merchandising to the present day.

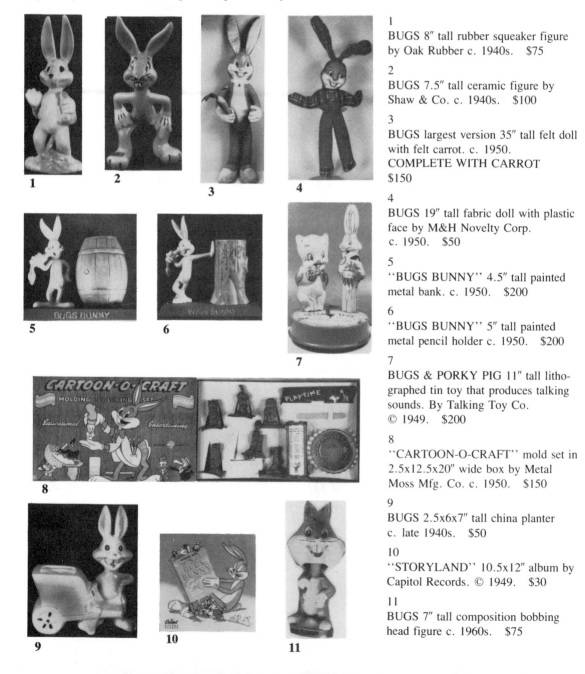

1
BUGS 8″ tall rubber squeaker figure by Oak Rubber c. 1940s. $75

2
BUGS 7.5″ tall ceramic figure by Shaw & Co. c. 1940s. $100

3
BUGS largest version 35″ tall felt doll with felt carrot. c. 1950.
COMPLETE WITH CARROT
$150

4
BUGS 19″ tall fabric doll with plastic face by M&H Novelty Corp.
c. 1950. $50

5
''BUGS BUNNY'' 4.5″ tall painted metal bank. c. 1950. $200

6
''BUGS BUNNY'' 5″ tall painted metal pencil holder c. 1950. $200

7
BUGS & PORKY PIG 11″ tall lithographed tin toy that produces talking sounds. By Talking Toy Co.
© 1949. $200

8
''CARTOON-O-CRAFT'' mold set in 2.5x12.5x20″ wide box by Metal Moss Mfg. Co. c. 1950. $150

9
BUGS 2.5x6x7″ tall china planter c. late 1940s. $50

10
''STORYLAND'' 10.5x12″ album by Capitol Records. © 1949. $30

11
BUGS 7″ tall composition bobbing head figure c. 1960s. $75

12
BUGS 1.5x4x4.5″ tall animated wind-up alarm clock by Ingraham Co.
c. 1951. $300

13
BUGS wristwatch in 1x4x7″ tall box by Richie Prem © 1951.   BOXED $350, LOOSE $200

14
BUGS Large Feature Comic No. 8 by Dell © 1942. $350

15
BUGS All Pictures Comics Better Little Book #1496 by Whitman
© 1945. $30

16
BUGS All Pictures Comics book by Whitman © 1943. $45

17
BUGS 8.5x11.5″ Whitman paint book
© 1949. $25

18
BUGS 8x10″ premium picture from Dell Comics. c. 1940s. $30

19
BUGS 8x10″ premium picture from Dell Comics. c. 1940s. $30

20
BUGS 9x12.5″ Big Golden Book
© 1951. $20

21
BUGS 7x9″ glow picture
c. 1950. $20

22
BUGS BUNNY 4″ tall hard plastic cup c. 1960s. $12

23
BUGS 8″ tall ceramic cookie jar by McCoy c. 1971. $225

24
BUGS/SPEEDY GONZALES 3″ tall English-made white ceramic mug
c. early 1970s. $50

25
BUGS 10″ tall plastic figure by Dakin
© 1971. $25

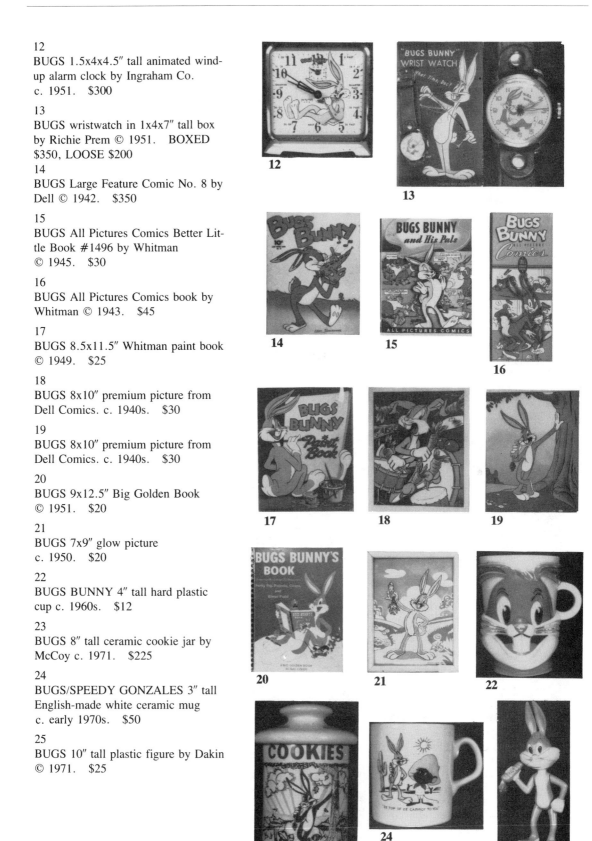

12

13

14

15

16

17

18

19

20

21

22

23

24

25

Buster Brown

Creator: Richard F. Outcault

Began: (S) 5/4/02, New York Herald.

Principal Characters: Buster Brown, his dog Tige, Mary Jane, Buddy Tucker.

Synopsis: A decided contrast character to Outcault's earlier comic character, The Yellow Kid, although both characters resulted in countless merchandise items. Buster Brown became associated almost immediately with clothing, and particularly shoe manufacturers. An updated Buster Brown headed a 1940s radio show, and Buster Brown children's shoes continued to be available into the 1990s.

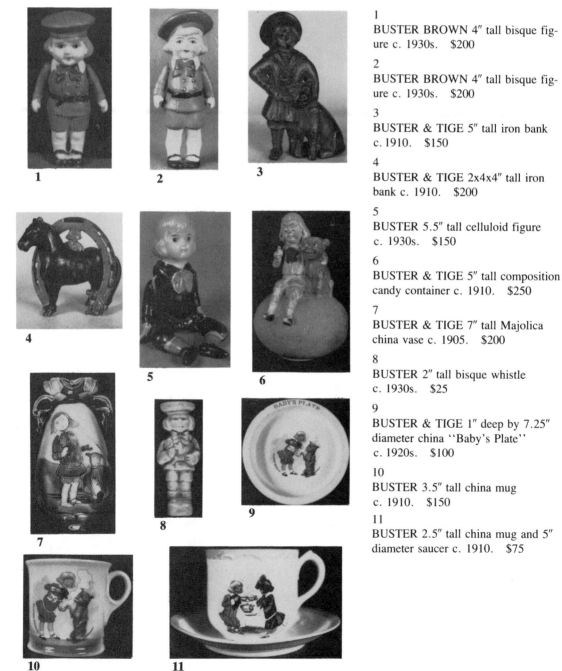

1
BUSTER BROWN 4″ tall bisque figure c. 1930s. $200

2
BUSTER BROWN 4″ tall bisque figure c. 1930s. $200

3
BUSTER & TIGE 5″ tall iron bank c. 1910. $150

4
BUSTER & TIGE 2x4x4″ tall iron bank c. 1910. $200

5
BUSTER 5.5″ tall celluloid figure c. 1930s. $150

6
BUSTER & TIGE 5″ tall composition candy container c. 1910. $250

7
BUSTER & TIGE 7″ tall Majolica china vase c. 1905. $200

8
BUSTER 2″ tall bisque whistle c. 1930s. $25

9
BUSTER & TIGE 1″ deep by 7.25″ diameter china ''Baby's Plate'' c. 1920s. $100

10
BUSTER 3.5″ tall china mug c. 1910. $150

11
BUSTER 2.5″ tall china mug and 5″ diameter saucer c. 1910. $75

12
"BROWN'S BLUE RIBBON" 4x6"
premium of jokes and jingles. Outcault characters Little Mose, Buddy
Tucker's Bear, Yellow Kid.
© 1904. $100

13
"BUSTER & TIGE 11x17" book of
newspaper strip reprints by Stokes Co.
© 1904. $150

14
BUSTER & PETS 10.5x16" book of
comic strip reprints c. 1905. $150

15
BUSTER IN FOREIGN LANDS
11x16" book of comic strip reprints by
Cupples & Leon Co. © 1912. $150

16
BUSTER'S PAINT BOOK" 10x14"
by Stokes Co. © 1907. $100

17
BUSTER 5.5x8" booklet of stories,
puzzles, jokes and art. March 1906
publication date. $75

18
"POND'S EXTRACT" 4.5x6.5"
booklet by maker of liquid pain killer
© 1904. $60

19
BUSTER ABROAD 8x10.25" book
by Stokes Co. © 1904. $100

20
BUSTER & DONKEY 6x8" Saalfield
cloth book © 1907. $65

21
BUSTER PLAYS INDIAN 6.5x7.5"
book from series Buster Brown Nug-
gets by Cupples & Leon Co.
© 1907. $75

22
BUSTER DISTURBS THE FAMILY
5.5x6.5" book by Stokes Co.
© 1917. $125

23

24

25

26

27

28

29

23
BUSTER BROWN 8x11″ musical stage show souvenir program c. early 1900s including photos of cast members plus Outcault art. $85

24
"BUSTER BROWN BREAD" 3.5x5.5″ trade card with full color art although not by Outcault. c. 1910. $75

25
BUSTER BROWN 4x6″ Christmas ad postcard with full color art including Dec. 1912 calendar. $25

26
BUSTER BROWN 3.5x5.5″ postcard No. 1 from series of 10 with full color Outcault art published by Burr McIntosh titled "Buster Brown And His Bubble" © 1903. $35

27
"BUSTER BROWN SHOES" 7.5x10″ wide full color paper half-mask with ad text on reverse. c. 1905. $75

28
"BUSTER BROWN NECKTIE PARTY" children's party game with object of blindfolded participant placing necktie on proper location of Buster's neck. Target is 24x30″ full color printed cheesecloth that includes 12 uncut necktie pieces. Game is folded into 7.5x10″ bwr cardboard cover shown in example photo with detail from the target.   Publisher is Selchow & Righter c. early 1900s.   BOXED $200, LOOSE $150, CUT $100

29
"BUSTER BROWN & TIGE PAPERDOLL" kit in 6.5x12.5″ bw cover envelope. Buster doll is 12″ tall in full color plus full color clothing items. Early 1900s. $125

30
"BUSTER BROWN CAMERA"
4x4x6″ wide full color carton only that
original held standard early snapshot
camera. $200

31
"BUSTER BROWN STOCKING
PAINT BOX" 4x5.5″ bwr cardboard
folder containing packet of pictures to
color. c. 1908. $75

32
BUSTER BROWN & TIGE 22x22″
fabric pillow cover. Captions are related to Buster's resolution to milk a
cow. Early 1900s. $200

33
"BUSTER BROWN MIXED PICK-
LING SPICES" 5″ tall by 3″ diameter
cardboard canister c. 1900s. $75

34
"BUSTER BROWN AT THE CIR-
CUS" card game in 4x5″ tall box by
Selchow & Righter. Early 1900s.
BOXED $175, COMPLETE
BUT LOOSE $100

35
"BUSTER BROWN GANG" 20x23″
fabric bandana radio show premium in
green, orange and black on white
background. Photo shows bandana
plus detail from it of Froggy The
Gremlin and Squeakie Mouse c. 1946-
1950. $85

36
FROGGY THE GREMLIN hollow
soft rubber squeaker toy produced in
both 9″ and 5″ heights c. 1948 by
Rempel Toys. LARGE SIZE $175,
SMALL SIZE $150

37
"FROGGY THE GREMLIN" 8x10″
diecut paper full color mask c. 1946
Ed McConnell copyright. $40

38
"BUSTER BROWN" wristwatch
c. 1975. $75

30

31   **32**   **33**

34

35

36   **37**   **38**

Charlie Chan

Creator: Alfred Andriola.

Began: (D) (S) 10/38. McNaught Syndicate.

Principal Characters: Charlie Chan, co-investigator Kirk Barrow, Number One Son Lee, Barrow's girlfriend Gina Lane.

Synopsis: Strip featuring the Oriental sleuth suggested by Earl Derr Biggers novels as well as a movie series starring Warner Oland or Sidney Toler. Chan's successes in solving cases of espionage. sabotage, spy activities were also detailed in sporadic comic book series between the late 1930s and mid-1960s. The original newspaper strip ceased in the spring of 1942.

1

2

3

1

"INSPECTOR CHARLIE CHAN OF THE HONOLULU POLICE" Whitman Better Little Book #1478 © 1939. $75

2

"CHARLIE CHAN SOLVES A NEW MYSTERY" Whitman Better Little Book #1459 © 1940. $60

3

"INSPECTOR CHARLIE CHAN/ VILLAINY ON THE HIGH SEAS" Whitman Better Little Book #1424 © 1942. $60

4

"CHARLIE CHAN" Whitman card game © 1939 with 35 playing cards plus instruction card in 1x5x6.5″ tall box. Photo example shows box lid and two playing cards. $75

5

"THE GREAT CHARLIE CHAN DETECTIVE MYSTERY GAME" by Milton Bradley Co. © 1937 in 2x11.5x22.5″ wide box. $150

6

"CHARLIE CHAN IN PANAMA" 6x9″ movie herald c. late 1930s. $25

7

"CHARLIE CHAN IN THE SECRET SERVICE" 22x28″ half-sheet film poster c. late 1930s. $50

5

6

7

Charlie Chaplin's Comic Capers

Creator: Various artists/writers including Elzie Segar.

Began: (D) (S) 1915. Chicago Record-Herald.

Principal Characters: Charlie Chaplin, Luke the Gook, Brutis.

Synopsis: Basically known as a silent film comedian, Chaplin's immense popularity resulted in comic panel strip books in the World War I era, as well as other collectibles from then until the present day. The strip itself was short-lived, ending in September 1917.

1
CHAPLIN COMIC CAPERS 10x16″ comic strip book by Donohue. © 1917. $100

2
CHAPLIN FUNNY STUNTS 12.5x16.5″ book by Donohue. © 1917. $75

3
UP IN THE AIR 10x17″ book by Donohue. © 1917. $75

4
IN THE ARMY 9x16″ book by Donohue. © 1917. $75

5
IN THE MOVIES 10x17″ book by Donohue. © 1917. $75

6
"LIBERTY GUN FOR YOUNG AMERICA" 7″ long cardboard store ad c. 1917. $40

7
CHAPLIN COLORING BOOK 11x15″ by Saalfield © 1941. $75

8
CHAPLIN WALK 10x14″ music © 1915. $30

9
CHAPLIN FEET 10x14″ music © 1915. $30

10
CHAPLIN 9″ tall painted plaster figure © 1915. $100

11
CHAPLIN 6.5″ tall tin wind-up. c. 1920s. $450

12
CHAPLIN 4.5″ tall bw cardboard figure c. 1920 or earlier. $35

1

2

3

4

5

6

7

8

9

10

11

12

The Cisco Kid

Creator: Jose Luis Salinas (artist), Rod Reed (writer)

Began: 1/1/51. King Features Syndicate.

Principal Characters: Cisco Kid, sidekick Pancho.

Synopsis: Western adventure strip prompted by 1920s-1940s movie versions followed by television series beginning in 1950. The television series returned Duncan Renaldo to the title role from his 1945 movie. Most of the merchandise items are based on the TV series costarring Leo Carillo as sidekick Pancho, rather than the concurrent comic strip version. The newspaper strip ceased in 1968.

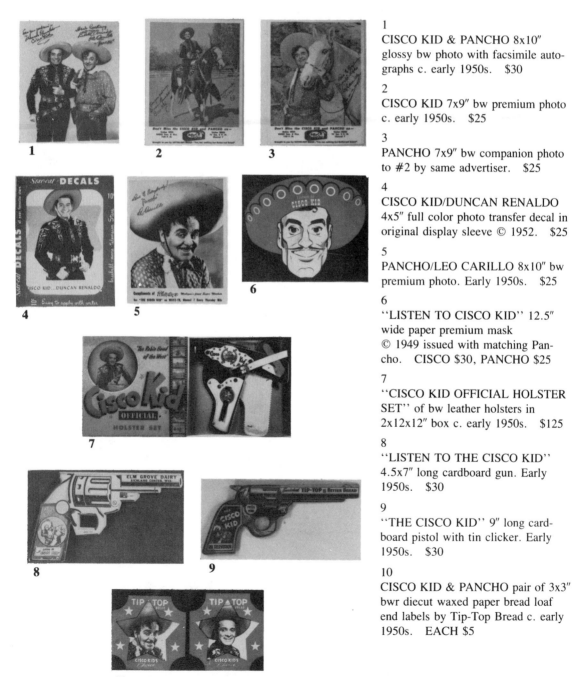

1
CISCO KID & PANCHO 8x10″ glossy bw photo with facsimile autographs c. early 1950s. $30

2
CISCO KID 7x9″ bw premium photo c. early 1950s. $25

3
PANCHO 7x9″ bw companion photo to #2 by same advertiser. $25

4
CISCO KID/DUNCAN RENALDO 4x5″ full color photo transfer decal in original display sleeve © 1952. $25

5
PANCHO/LEO CARILLO 8x10″ bw premium photo. Early 1950s. $25

6
"LISTEN TO CISCO KID" 12.5″ wide paper premium mask © 1949 issued with matching Pancho.   CISCO $30, PANCHO $25

7
"CISCO KID OFFICIAL HOLSTER SET" of bw leather holsters in 2x12x12″ box c. early 1950s. $125

8
"LISTEN TO THE CISCO KID" 4.5x7″ long cardboard gun. Early 1950s. $30

9
"THE CISCO KID" 9″ long cardboard pistol with tin clicker. Early 1950s. $30

10
CISCO KID & PANCHO pair of 3x3″ bwr diecut waxed paper bread loaf end labels by Tip-Top Bread c. early 1950s.   EACH $5

11
"TV DIGEST" 5.25x7.5" forerunner edition to TV Guide for Philadelphia area in 1951 with Cisco Kid cover art. $20

12
"CATTLE BRANDS" 7.5x10" premium booklet c. early 1950s. $75

13
"CISCO KID RODEO" 8.5x11" program c. early 1950s. $25

14
"CISCO KID COLORING BOOK" 11x14" by Saalfield © 1950. $35

15
CISCO KID AND PANCHO COLORING BOOK 11x15" by Saalfield © 1950. $35

16
"COMIC ALBUM" 7x10" English-published book c. 1950s. $20

17
DUNCAN RENALDO 8x10" school tablet. Early 1950s. $20

18
RENALDO/CISCO 8x10" school tablet c. 1950. $20

19
CARILLO/PANCHO 8x10" school tablet c. 1950. $20

20
CISCO KID 10x11" Saalfield tray puzzle c. 1951. $30

21
THE CISCO KID 10x11" Saalfield tray puzzle © 1951. $25

22
CISCO/PANCHO 10x11" Saalfield tray puzzle © 1951. $25

23
CISCO/DIABLO puzzle by Saalfield in 7x10x2" deep box. 1950s. $25

24
CISCO KID 7x13" cardboard sign for Lay's Potato Chips. Early 1950s. $45

11

12

13

14

15

16

17

18

19

20

21

22

23

24

Dan Dunn

Creator: Norman Marsh

Began: (D) 10/16/33; (S) 10/22/33. Publishers Newspaper Syndicate.

Later Artists and/or Writers: Paul Pinson, Alfred Andriola.

Principal Characters: Dan Dunn, his dog Wolf, Babs, Irwin Higgs, Wu Fang, Spider Slick, Eviloff.

Synopsis: Detective strip created to draw popularity from the Dick Tracy strip begun in 1931. Although Dunn indeed drew his following, the merchandise items for him consisted almost entirely of books as opposed to the much wider range of Tracy artifacts. The strip ceased in 1943.

1

DAN DUNN "I'M OPERATIVE 48" 1¼" orange/purple/fleshtone/bw cello pin-back button from comic character series of 1930s issued by (Philadelphia) Evening Ledger Comics with back paper ad text. $75

2

DAN DUNN 3x3" Whitman Buddy Book #6 © 1938 offered as premium for ice cream cone coupons. $40

3

DAN DUNN 2.5x3.75" Whitman Penny Book © 1938. $15

4

DAN DUNN 4x5.5" Dell Fast-Action Book © 1938. $50

5

DAN DUNN Whitman Big Little Book #1171 © 1937. $20

6

DAN DUNN Whitman Better Little Book #1492 © 1940. $30

7

DAN DUNN Whitman Big Little Book #1125 © 1936. $25

8

DAN DUNN Whitman Big Little Book #1454 © 1938. $25

9

DAN DUNN Whitman All-Pictures Comics © 1941. $25

10

DAN DUNN Whitman Big Little Book #1118 © 1936. $25

Dennis the Menace

Creator: Hank Ketcham

Began: (D) 3/12/51, (S) 1952. Hall Syndicate.

Principal Characters: Dennis Mitchell, parents Henry and Alice Mitchell, dog Ruff, Margaret, Joey, next-door neighbor Mr. Wilson.

Synopsis: Single panel humor cartoon centered around the mischievous, devilish antics of a five-year-old tyke. Most merchandise items are based on the Dennis character of Ketcham's strips although a few others resulted from the 1959-1963 live action television series starring Jay North in the title role.

1
DENNIS & RUFF 3.5x4.5x7″ tall vinyl electrical night lamp
© 1960. $90

2
DENNIS 7.5″ tall full color painted hollow soft vinyl figure
© 1959. $60

3
DENNIS 10″ tall cloth doll with hard fabric painted face, yellow string hair, colorful fabric outfit, wooden feet.
c. 1950s. $50

4
DENNIS 10″ tall character hand puppets, each with soft vinyl head and fabric hand cover body. c. 1950s. EACH $25

5
DENNIS 5.5″ tall painted hard plastic figure toy with arm that raises holding pistol which squirts water. Toy is in 2.5x3.5x6″ tall box. © 1954. $50

6
DENNIS STUFF N' LACE DOLL cloth assembly kit in 1.5x10x15″ tall box. By Standard Toykraft c. 1950s. $30

7
DENNIS 4″ tall colorfully painted hard plastic mug c. 1950s. $15

8
DENNIS 6.25x9.25″ first edition hard cover book published by Holt & Co. with 64 pages of bw single panel cartoons. $15

9
DENNIS MISCHIEF KIT by Hasbro Co. in 2x11.5x15.5″ wide box with props for various tricks including bugs, snake bow tie, replica ink blot, etc. © 1955. $45

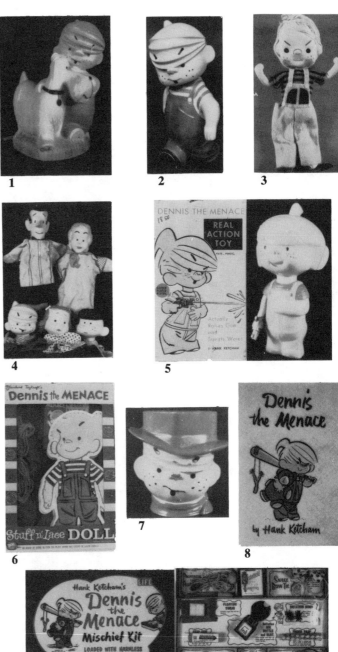

Dick Tracy

Creator: Chester Gould

Began: (S) 10/4/31; (D) 10/12/31. Chicago Tribune-New York News Syndicate.

Principal Characters: Dick Tracy, Tess Trueheart, Junior Tracy, Pat Patton, Bonny Braids, Gravel Gertie, B. O. Plenty, Sparkle Plenty, a host of villains over the years.

Synopsis: The quintessential detective strip for three decades followed by a shift to space age crimefighting through most of the 1960s. In addition to the comic strip, Tracy has been portrayed in about six films of the late 1930s-early 1940s; both live action and animated television series in the 1950s-1960s; and the 1990 full length film version. Each produced hundreds of Tracy collectibles.

1
DICK TRACY 6x8″ full color picture. 1930s. $125

2
DICK TRACY 5x7.5″ booklet by Quaker Cereals © 1939. $60

3
DICK TRACY 1 ⅝″ button c. 1938. $25

4
DICK TRACY 3x6″ Quaker Cereals booklet c. 1938. $40

5
DICK TRACY 2x3″ brass belt badge with attached leather pouch. 1930s. $75

6
DICK TRACY 7″ long   cardboard gun c. 1930s. $35

7
DICK TRACY 6.5″ long cardboard gun © 1944. $45

8
DICK TRACY 8x10.5″ booklet by Miller Bros. Hat Co. 1930s. $150

9
DICK TRACY elastic suspenders in 12″ tall box. c. 1940s. $100

10
''DICK TRACY CRIMESTOPPERS CLUB'' kit in 9″ tall plain carton c. 1961. $25

11
DICK TRACY DETECTIVE SET in
2x9x15″ wide box by Pressman Co.
c. 1930s. $100

12
DICK TRACY 17″ diameter cardboard
target by Marx. 1930s. $75

13
"MUGG & TRACY" 9x9″ china
plate c. 1940s. $75

14
DICK TRACY RIOT CAR 3x3x7″ tin
Marx Co. friction toy designed to
shoot sparks. In original gw box.
1930s. $150

15
DICK TRACY POLICE CAR 3x4x8″
tin battery operated remote control toy
vehicle in 3.25x6x9″ wide box. By
Linemar Toys © 1949. $750

16
"DICK TRACY WATCH" by New
Haven Time Co. in 1x3x5″ tall box
with original papers c. 1947. BOXED
$300, LOOSE $100

17
"DICK TRACY SIREN POLICE
PISTOL" by Marx in 2x4x9″ box
© 1934.   BOXED $200, LOOSE
$100

18
DICK TRACY 3″ tall painted glass
tree lightbulb c. 1930s. $40

19
DICK TRACY paper "Hingees" kit
in 7.5x11.5″ full color envelope.
© 1945. $50

20
"B.O. PLENTY" 8″ tall full color
lithographed tin wind-up. When acti-
vated, toy rocks back and forth as tin
hat raises and lowers. By Marx Toys
c. late 1940s. $200

21
DICK TRACY 11″ tall hand puppet
© 1962. $45

22
"DICK TRACY IN MOVIE STYLE"
hand viewer and bw films in 2x5x7.5″
wide box © 1953. $100

11

12   **13**   **14**

15

16   **17**   **18**

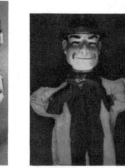

19   **20**   **21**

22

23

25

26

27

28

29

30

31

32

33

34

35

36

23
DICK TRACY ''PILLSBURY'S
COMICOOKY BAKING SET'' in
1x5x7″ tall box. © 1937. $75

24
NEW YORK SUNDAY NEWS
11x17″ rwb/yellow cardboard poster
c.1933. $200

25
DICK TRACY PAINT BOOK 11x14″
Whitman book © 1935. $90

26
DICK TRACY 7x8.5″ book by Cupples & Leon Co. with 86 pages.
© 1933. $150

27
DICK TRACY 3x5″ Dell Fast-Action
Book © 1941. $75

28
DICK TRACY 3.5x3.5″ Quaker Cereals booklet c. 1939. $40

29
DICK TRACY Whitman Big Little
Book #710 © 1933. $100

30
DICK TRACY Whitman Big Little
Book © 1933. $75

31
DICK TRACY Dell Large Feature
Comic #8 from 1938, the first featur-
ing Tracy. $265

32
DICK TRACY Dell Four Color
Comic #1 (no number) from Series 1
in 1939. $900

33
DICK TRACY 5.5x8″ Whitman book
© 1943 with dust jacket. $15

34
DICK TRACY CARD GAME   by
Whitman © 1937 in 5x6.5″ box. $50

35
DICK TRACY CARD GAME by
Whitman © 1941 in 5x6.5″ box. $50

36
DICK TRACY CARD GAME by
Whitman © 1934 in 5x6.5″ box. $50

37

"DICK TRACY CANDY AND
TOY" 1x2.5x3.75" wide box with full
color art on top and sides plus rwb/
yellow four-panel comic strip on bottom panel to be torn from box for use
as "Play Card" 11 from a series by
Novel Package Co. c. 1940s. $125

37

38

"DICK TRACY BIG LITTLE BOOK
PICTURE PUZZLES" Whitman set
of two puzzles © 1938 in 8x10x2" tall
box. $90

39

"DICK TRACY 2-WAY ELEC-
TRONIC WRIST RADIOS" set of
plastic battery operated wrist units in
2.5x9.5x13.5" wide box. By Remco
Industries c. 1950s. $125

40

"DICK TRACY" model kit by Aurora Plastics Co. in 1.5x5x13" tall
box. © 1968. $100

38

39

40

41

"DICK TRACY'S BONNY
BRAIDS" 1.25" figural plastic pin on
full color 3.5x5.5" card © 1951. $35

42

"BONNY BRAIDS PAPERDOLLS"
10x12" Saalfield book © 1951 also including a Tess Trueheart doll plus uncut clothing. $65

43

"BONNY BRAIDS PAPERDOLLS"
10x12" Saalfield book © 1951 also including Tess Trueheart dolls with uncut clothing. $65

41

42

43

44

"DICK TRACY" 7x8x4" deep embossed steel lunch box with 6.5" tall
steel bottle, not shown in photo example. By Aladdin Industries © 1967.
BOX $125, BOTTLE $50

44

45

DICK TRACY "SUNDAY FUN-
NIES" game by Ideal Toy Corp.
© 1972 in 1.5x12x15.5" tall
box. $20

46

DICK TRACY "SOAKY" 10" tall
plastic soap container c. 1960s. $25

45

46

Donald Duck

Creator: Walt Disney Studios

Later Artists and/or Writers: Al Taliaferro, Bob Karp and others.

Principal Characters: Donald Duck, Daisy Duck, nephews Dewey, Huey and Louie; later, Uncle Scrooge, Ludwig Von Drake.

Synopsis: Donald was introduced briefly in comic strip art late in 1934 as a visitor to Mickey Mouse and other Disney character strips. After a few other brief mid-1930s appearances, Donald's strip began in its own right as a daily in 1938. Donald has appeared regularly in other print and animated media over the years, resulting in hundreds of collectibles.

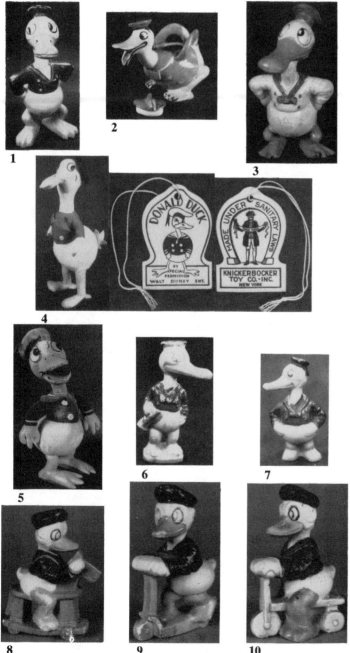

1
DONALD 4x5x8.5″ tall painted and jointed composition figure by Knickerbocker Toys c. 1935. $500

2
DONALD 3x4″ tall by 5.5″ long china creamer by Wadeheath of England c. 1935. $350

3
DONALD 4.75″ tall rubber figure by Seiberling Rubber Co. c. 1935, also known in larger 6″ size.   SMALL SIZE $200, LARGE SIZE $300

4
DONALD 13″ tall cloth doll by Knickerbocker with string tag c. 1935.   WITH TAG $300, WITHOUT $250

5
DONALD 15″ tall stuffed doll of velveteen and oilcloth by Richard Krueger Co. c. 1936. $300

6
DONALD 3″ tall painted bisque figure c. 1935. $60

7
DONALD 2″ tall painted bisque figure with long bill c. 1935. $45

8
DONALD ON ROCKING HORSE 3.25″ tall painted bisque figure c. 1940. $100

9
DONALD ON SCOOTER 3.25″ tall painted bisque figure c. 1940. $100

10
DONALD ON TRICYCLE 3.25″ tall painted bisque figure c. 1940. $100

11
ADMIRAL DONALD & SAILOR
NEPHEW painted bisque figure set c.
1939. Donald is 3″ tall and nephew is
2″. DONALD $75, NEPHEW $25

12
DONALD 3.25″ tall painted bisque
figure c. 1935. $35

13
DONALD 3.5x3.5x4″ long ceramic
figure depicted with angry expression.
By Brayton Laguna Pottery
c. 1940. $200

14
DONALD 6.5″ tall ceramic figure de-
picted with angry expression. By
American Pottery Co. c. 1947. $150

15
DONALD 11″ tall china cookie jar in
seated position by American Bisque
Co. c. 1940s. $150

16
DONALD 13″ tall ceramic cookie jar
in standing position by Leeds China
Co. c. 1940s. $200

17
DONALD 9″ long painted celluloid
wind-up toy in 3x5.5x9.5″ box.
c. 1934. BOXED $1200,
UNBOXED $750

18
DONALD 4.5″ tall celluloid acrobat
figure on wire trapeze bar stand. Distributed by George Borgfeldt Corp. c.
1935. Box is 2x6x9″ tall. BOXED
$1500, UNBOXED $1000

19
DONALD & PLUTO RAIL CAR of
composition and metal wind-up by
Lionel Corp. c. 1936. $750

20
DONALD 5″ tall tin wind-up by
Schuco Toys. c. 1935. $1000

21
DONALD 5″ tall celluloid wind-up in
3x4x6″ wide box. Distributed by
George Bordfeldt Corp. c. 1935.
BOXED $1500, UNBOXED $1000

11

12

13

14

15

16

17

18

19

20   **21**

22

23

24

25

26

27

28

29

30

31

32   **33**

22
DONALD 7″ tall wood pull toy by
Fisher-Price c. 1936. $350

23
DONALD ''CHOO-CHOO'' 8″ long
wood pull toy by Fisher-Price
c. 1942. $150

24
DONALD 10″ long wood pull toy by
Fisher-Price c. 1941. $150

25
DONALD 13″ tall wood pull toy with
metal xylophone by Fisher-Price
c. 1946. $200

26
''DONALD DUCK'' 2.5x3.5x6.5″
long rubber car by Sun Rubber Co.
c. 1940s. $50

27
DONALD 4x5x5″ tall rubber tractor
toy by Sun Rubber Co.
c. 1940s. $50

28
''THE WISE LITTLE HEN'' 9.5x13″
Whitman book #888 with 1934 story
which introduced Donald Duck
© 1937. $85

29
''DONALD DUCK'' 9x13″ book by
Whitman, the first book devoted to
him © 1935. $175

30
FIRST DONALD COMIC BOOK
published by Whitman/K.K. Publications © 1938. $325

31
''THE DONALD DUCK BOOK''
7x10″ by Birn Bros., England
c. 1937. $200

32
''MICKEY MOUSE MAGAZINE''
Vol. 1 #8, with second solo appearance of Donald. By K.K. Publica-
tions/Western Publishing Co. May
1936. $145

33
''DONALD'S LUCKY DAY''
9.5x11.5″ book by Whitman
© 1939. $125

34
DONALD 8.5x11.5″ Whitman book
© 1937. $150

35
"THE LIFE OF DONALD DUCK"
8.5x11″ book. Published in Australia
by John Sands. © 1941. $125

36
"WALT DISNEY'S PAINT BOOK"
11x15″ book by Whitman with 48
pages © 1949. $60

37
"DONALD DUCK'S ATOM
BOMB" pocket size Cheerios comic
with art by Carl Barks © 1947.
$115

38
DONALD DUCK 7x9″ studio fan card
with facsimile Disney signature.
c. 1940s. $250

39
DONALD DUCK 4x5″ full color studio Christmas card c. 1940s. $85

40
"DONALD DUCK" 5.5x9″ school
pencil tablet with full color cover art.
By Powers Paper Co. © 1937. $75

41
"DONALD DUCK BEAN BAG
PARTY GAME" by Parker Brothers
in 2x13x19″ tall box c. 1940s.
BOXED $150, BOARD
ONLY $75

42
DONALD & NEPHEW 7x12″ diecut
full color cardboard store sign for Sylvania Radio Tubes © 1941. $300

43
"DONALD DUCK DIME REGIS-
TER BANK" .75x2.5x2.5″ tin bank.
© 1939. $250

44
DONALD DUCK 2x4.5x4.5″ tall
wind-up alarm clock by Reveils Bayard of France c. 1965. $175

45
DONALD DUCK WRISTWATCH by
Ingersoll in 1x4x7″ box by US Time.
c. 1947. BOXED $400, UNBOXED
$200

34

35

36

37

38

39

40

41

42

43

44

45

Don Winslow

Creator: Lt. Commander Frank V. Martinek (writer), Leon Beroth and Carl Hammond (artists)

Began: (D) 3/5/34; (S) 1935. Bell Syndicate.

Later Artists and/or Writers: Ken Ernst, Ed Moore, Al Levin.

Principal Characters: Lt. Commander Don Winslow, partner Lt. Red Pennington, Admiral Colby, Mercedes Colby, arch-rival Scorpion.

Synopsis: Originally titled Don Winslow of the Navy, the strip resulted from Martinek novels designed to aid U.S. Naval recruiting. The strip, generally involving stories of Winslow vs. spies and espionage agents, flourished during the World War II era and was the basis of two early 1940s serial movies. Newspaper publication ceased in 1955.

1

2

3

4

5

6

7

8

9

10

1
DON WINSLOW Fawcett comic book #50 for October 1947. $20

2
DON WINSLOW "SUPER BOOK OF COMICS" Western Publishing Co. comic book #6 c. 1945. $40

3
DON WINSLOW 5.5x8″ Whitman book #2327 with dust jacket. © 1946. $15

4
DON WINSLOW 2.5x3.75″ Whitman Penny Book © 1938. $15

5
DON WINSLOW Whitman Better Little Book #1418 © 1942. $30

6
DON WINSLOW Whitman Better Little Book #1419 © 1938. $30

7
DON WINSLOW Whitman unnumbered Better Little Book © 1946. $25

8
DON WINSLOW Whitman Better Little Book #1489 © 1940. $25

9
WINSLOW "FAVORITE FUNNIES" 1.5x6x8″ long boxed puzzle by Jaymar c. 1940s. $35

10
"THE DON WINSLOW PERISCOPE" 2x2x17″ tall cardboard viewer. Kellogg Cereal premium c. 1939. $100

11
DON WINSLOW 7.5″ tall painted plaster figurine c. mid-1940s. $25

12
"DON WINSLOW" & "RED PENNINGTON" painted plaster salt and pepper set with Winslow figure slightly taller 3″. 1940s. SET $50

13
DON WINSLOW 5.5x8″ Grosset & Dunlap book with dust jacket. © 1941. $15

14
DON WINSLOW 4x8″ manual. © 1935. $70

15
"DON WINSLOW MAGIC SLATE" 4x6.5″ manual with 16 pages plus erasable film slate and wood stylus. © 1953. $40

16
"DON WINSLOW BREAKING THE SOUND BARRIER" 4x7″ magic slate booklet with 32-page story c. 1950s. $40

17
DON WINSLOW "ENSIGN" 3/4″ metal Kellogg's premium c. 1939. $25

18
"DON WINSLOW'S OFFICIAL SQUADRON OF PEACE MANUAL" 4.75x6.25″ Kellogg's handbook from 1939. $50

19
"DON WINSLOW CREED" 6.25x9.5″ rwb paper creed sheet for Squadron of Peace member. Kellogg Cereal premium c. 1939. $25

20
DON WINSLOW "GUARDIANS OF PEACE" 6x8″ back panel from Kellogg's Wheat Krispies series. Example photo is of "Destroyer Mahan." © 1938. $15

21
"DON WINSLOW'S TATTOO TRANSFERS" 5x7.5″ packet of full color water transfer pictures plus unrelated small games and puzzles. Coco-Wheats premium c. 1956 in original 6x9″ mailing envelope. $50

11

12

13

14

15

16

17

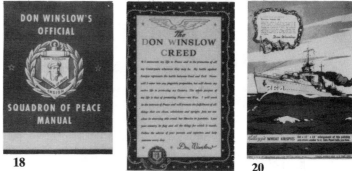

18

19

20

21

Felix the Cat

Creator: Pat Sullivan, Otto Messmer

Began: (S) 8/12/23; (D) 5/9/27. King Features Syndicate.

Principal Characters: Felix the Cat, fickle girlfriend Phyllis.

Synopsis: Felix had acquired considerable fame as an early animated silent cartoon star before his introduction in newspaper comic strips. Among his characteristics are his frequent ''walking'' posture with arms clasped behind, plus a tail of many talents and functions. His destiny since the mid-1950s has been guided by Joe Oriolo Studios. The concept of Felix as the plucky loner remains popular to the present.

1
FELIX largest size 7.5″ tall Schoenhut jointed wood doll © 1924 decal. $250

2
FELIX 5.5″ tall Schoenhut jointed wood figure © 1924. $100

3
FELIX 3.25″ tall wood figure with green body c. 1930s. $225

4
FELIX 13″ tall composition figure © 1924. $400

5
FELIX 5.25″ tall cardboard and wood ramp walker figure © 1924. $350

6
FELIX 2″ tall metal figure with spring-mounted head c. 1920s. $300

7
FELIX 3.5″ tall celluloid figure c. 1930s. $200

8
FELIX 3″ tall hollow celluloid figure c. 1930s. $100

9
FELIX 2.5″ tall painted iron figure c. 1930s. $250

10
FELIX 8″ long tin wind-up toy c. 1930. $600

11
FELIX 2.25″ diameter palm puzzle c. 1930s. $75

12
FELIX 4x5″ tin license plate attachment c. 1940s. $150

13
FELIX 12″ tall English cloth doll
c. 1930s. $150

14
FELIX 5.5″ tall metal sparkler toy
c. 1930s. $300

15
FELIX 4.75″ tall plaster figure with
rhinestone eyes. c. 1930s. $400

16
FELIX 6.5″ tall metal bank
© 1939. $300

17
"FELIX" 6.5″ tall wood figure
c. 1930s. $250

18
FELIX 2.5″ tall painted lead figure on
base c. 1930s. $200

19
FELIX 1.5″ tall celluloid tape measure
c. 1930s. $300

20
FELIX 2.5x4.25″ tall diecut celluloid
bookmark c. 1930s. $150

21
FELIX 2″ tall tin musical toy also picturing Mickey and Minnie Mouse
c. 1930s. $350

22
FELIX 7″ china plate by Rudolstadt,
Germany © 1925. $250

23
FELIX china tea set by Villeroy &
Boch consisting of 5″ tall teapot and
accessory pieces. c. 1930s.
TEAPOT $300, COVERED SUGAR
BOWL $150, CREAMER $150, CUP
& SAUCER $150

24
FELIX 6″ Limoges china plate
c. 1930s. $125

25
FELIX 2x2x2.25″ long Wilton white
china figurine c. 1920s. $175

26
FELIX 2.25″ tall Wilton china barrel
c. 1920s. $150

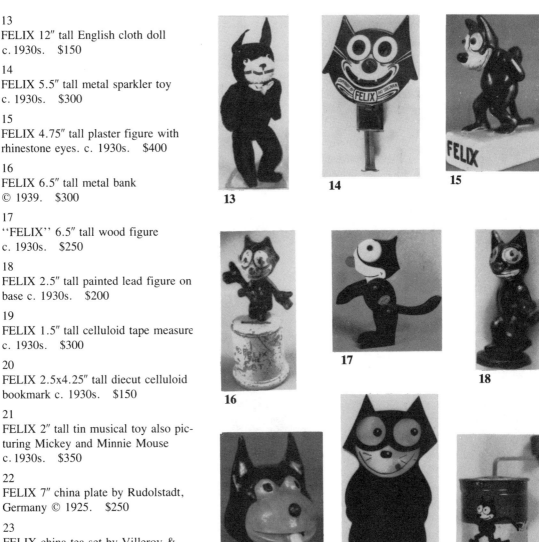

27

28

29

30

31

32

33

34

35

36

37

38

39

27
FELIX 1.5″ tall Wilton china vase
c. 1920s. $150

28
BABY FELIX 3.75″ tall china milk
pitcher c. 1930s. $150

29
''FELIX CREAM TOFFEE'' 4x6x6″
tall bwr lithographed tin candy box for
R. K. Confectionary Co. of England
c. 1920s. $1200

30
FELIX SIP-A-DRINK 5″ tall plastic
mug c. 1950s. $40

31
FELIX 10″ tall plastic ''Soaky'' soap
container c. 1960s. $40

32
FELIX 3.5x5.5″ postcard #4817 by
Florence House, London.
1920s. $25

33
''THE FELIX ANNUAL'' 7.5x10″
English book with back cover
Ovaltine ad. © 1925. $75

34
''THE FELIX ANNUAL'' 7.5x10″
English book with back cover
Ovaltine ad. 1920s. $100

35
FELIX 8x10.25″ book published by
McLoughlin Brothers © 1931. $350

36
FELIX 8x16″ book by McLoughlin
Brothers © 1927. $400

37
FELIX 6x8.5″ book by Henry Alte-
mus Co. © 1931. $150

38
FELIX THE CAT Whitman Big Little
Book #1129 © 1936. $75

39
FELIX Whitman All Pictures Better
Little Book #1465 © 1945. $60

40
"FELIX THE CAT" 10x12" sheet music © 1928 with cover art in yellow/blue/bw. $75

41
"FELIX KEPT ON WALKING" 10x12" English-published sheet music © 1923 with bw cover art. $50

42
FELIX & FRIEND 16x16" fabric pillow cover with full color art bordered by green squares. c. 1930s. $300

43
"FELIX" .5x5x8.5" wide textured red cardboard pencil case with bw art on lid and bottom. By American Pencil Co. c. 1930s. $100

44
"FELIX SCHOOL COMPANION" .5x4x8.25" wide textured green cardboard pencil case with lid art in silver. By American Pencil Co. © 1939. $100

45
"NAVY AIRCRAFT SQUADRON INSIGNIA" card game including pair of cards as issued picturing Felix as insignia of "Fighting Squadron No. 3." Game is by All-Fair Co. in 1x4x5" wide box. c. early 1940s. $100

46
"FELIX" original art by Otto Messmer for comic book on 15x20.5" white art sheet. Art is inked in black with © 1949 for use in Dell comic #7, page 5. $200

47
"FELIX ON TELEVISION" 6.5x8" "Flip-It Book" with full color art on cover plus 20-page story by Joe Oriolo. Page corners have small art to be flipped rapidly. Wonder Book © 1956. $30

48
"FELIX THE CAT" Milton Bradley game featuring full color playing board depicting Felix and eight friends plus deck of 24 Felix cards. Box is 1.5x8.5x16.5" wide with full color lid art. © 1960. $60

40

41

42

43

44

45

46

47

48

Flash Gordon

Creator: Alex Raymond (artist), Don Moore (writer)

Began: (S) 1/7/34; (D) 5/27/40. King Features Syndicate.

Later Artists and/or Writers: Austin Briggs, Mac Raboy, Dan Barry, Al Williamson, Frank Frazetta, Ray Krenkel, Ric Estrada.

Principal Characters: Flash Gordon, Dale Arden, Dr. Zarkov, arch-nemesis Ming the Merciless.

Synopsis: Very successful and enduring strip developed to compete with the science-fiction adventures of Buck Rogers. The battles between Flash and cohorts against Ming on the Planet Mongo have lasted over 50 years with both movie serial and radio versions in the 1930s plus later television versions in both live action and animated form.

1
"BUSTER CRABBE" 9x11" full color Dixie Ice Cream premium photo of him in Flash Gordon uniform from movie serial. Undated c. 1936. $100

2
"BUSTER CRABBE" 2.25" sepia Dixie Ice Cream waxed cardboard lid picturing him as Flash Gordon in film serial. Undated c. 1936. $30

3
LOOK 10.5x13.5" magazine with Flash Gordon cover article. March 15, 1938. $35

4
FLASH GORDON 11.5x14" Whitman paint book © 1936. $125

5
FLASH GORDON 8x9" "Pop-Up" Blue Ribbon Book © 1935. $250

6
FLASH GORDON 5.5x7.75" Grosset & Dunlap book with dust jacket. © 1936. $75

7
FLASH GORDON 4x5.5" Fast-Action Story book © 1942. $75

8
FLASH GORDON Whitman Big Little Book #1110 © 1934. $60

9
FLASH GORDON Whitman Big Little Book #1166 © 1935. $60

10
FLASH GORDON 10" long red metal "Air Ray Gun" in box by Budson Co. © 1948. BOXED $250, LOOSE $150

11
FLASH GORDON SIGNAL PISTOL
7″ long metal gun in box by Marx
Toys © 1935.   BOXED $500,
LOOSE $350

11

12
FLASH GORDON RADIO REPEA-
TER CLICK PISTOL 9.5″ long tin
gun in box by Marx Toys © 1935.
BOXED $300, LOOSE $200

12

13
FLASH GORDON CLICK RAY PIS-
TOL 10″ long gun in box by Marx
Toys c. early 1950s.   BOXED $350,
LOOSE $200

13

14
FLASH GORDON WATER PISTOL
7.5″ long plastic gun in box by Marx
Toys c. early 1950s.   BOXED $175,
LOOSE $100

14

15
"FLASH GORDON MOVIE CLUB"
3x4″ membership card numbered on
bottom margin 1 through 13 for ad-
mittance to serial chapters c. late
1930s. $400

15

16

16
FLASH GORDON ROCKET
FIGHTER 12″ long tin wind-up by
Marx Toys. 1939. $400

17
"FLASH GORDON-MARCH OF
COMICS" 5x7″ booklet #142
© 1956. $35

18
FLASH GORDON 1x5x6″ tall diecut
yellow foam bath sponge issued originally in 3x7″ pack with two other
comic character sponges. 1950s. $15

19
FLASH GORDON set of three 11x14″
full color puzzles in box by Milton
Bradley © 1951. $100

17

18

20
FLASH GORDON 1.5x9x18″ tall
boxed game by Game Gems
© 1965. $60

19   **20**

The Flintstones

Creator: Hanna-Barbera Studios.

Began: 1960 (CBS-TV) McNaught Syndicate 1961.

Later Artists and/or Writers: Gene Hazelton.

Principal Characters: Fred Flintstone, wife Wilma, neighbors Barney and Betty Rubble, pets Dino (dinosaur) and Baby Puss (tiger), youngsters Pebbles Flintstone and Bamm-Bamm Rubble.

Synopsis: Comic strip quickly evolved from the first animation series to appear on prime time television. Both featured contemporary comedy situations but located in the Stone Age community of Bedrock. Situations are typically slapstick variety involving Fred vs. Barney, both vs. wives. Fred's battle cry "Yabba Dabba Doo" inspired several commercial products.

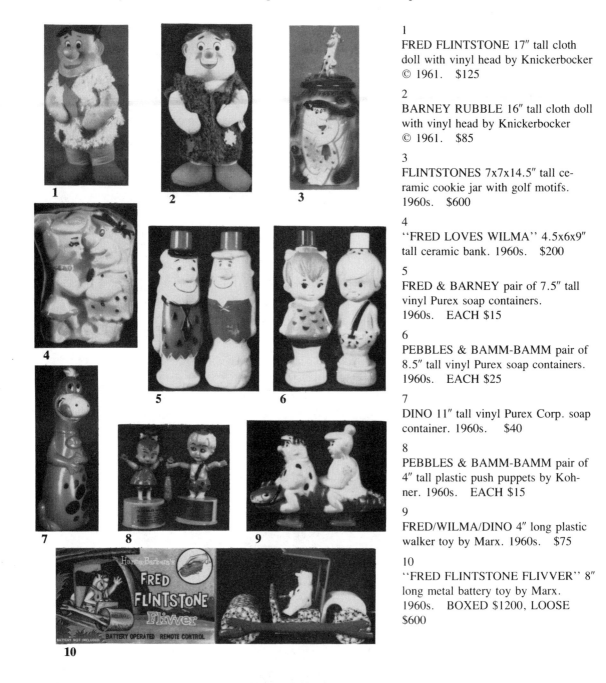

1
FRED FLINTSTONE 17" tall cloth doll with vinyl head by Knickerbocker © 1961. $125

2
BARNEY RUBBLE 16" tall cloth doll with vinyl head by Knickerbocker © 1961. $85

3
FLINTSTONES 7x7x14.5" tall ceramic cookie jar with golf motifs. 1960s. $600

4
"FRED LOVES WILMA" 4.5x6x9" tall ceramic bank. 1960s. $200

5
FRED & BARNEY pair of 7.5" tall vinyl Purex soap containers. 1960s.   EACH $15

6
PEBBLES & BAMM-BAMM pair of 8.5" tall vinyl Purex soap containers. 1960s.   EACH $25

7
DINO 11" tall vinyl Purex Corp. soap container. 1960s. $40

8
PEBBLES & BAMM-BAMM pair of 4" tall plastic push puppets by Kohner. 1960s.   EACH $15

9
FRED/WILMA/DINO 4" long plastic walker toy by Marx. 1960s. $75

10
"FRED FLINTSTONE FLIVVER" 8" long metal battery toy by Marx. 1960s.   BOXED $1200, LOOSE $600

11
"THE FLINTSTONES" 2.5x2.5x4"
long metal wind-up tank toy by Linemar Toys © 1961. $275

12
"BEDROCK EXPRESS/FLINT-
STONE CHOO-CHOO TRAIN" tin
wind-up toy by Marx. 1960s. $400

13
"FRED FLINTSTONE ON DINO"
7x12" tall by 21" long battery toy in
box. Walking Dino figure has vinyl
head and soft plush fabric overlay
body. By Marx Toys © 1962.
BOXED $600, UNBOXED $350

14
FRED ON DINO 2.5x5.5x8" long
metal wind-up walking toy by Marx
© 1962. $250

15
"FRED FLINTSTONE ZILO"
5x8x8" tall wood, metal and litho paper musical pull toy by Fisher-Price
© 1962. $250

16
FLINTSTONE 15" tall by 23" wide by
29" long plastic walking toy for use
by actual youngster. By AMF Corp.
c. late 1960s or 1970s. $90

17
"FLINTSTONES AND DINO"
7x8x4" deep full color steel lunch box
with 6.5" steel bottle. By Aladdin Industries © 1962.   BOX EMBOSSED
$75, BOX FLAT $125, BOTTLE $40

18
"THE FLINTSTONES" electrical table lamp with 9" tall plastic figure of
Fred as lamp stand. Lamp shade is 8"
tall by 9" diameter paper.
© 1960.   COMPLETE $175,
NO SHADE $100

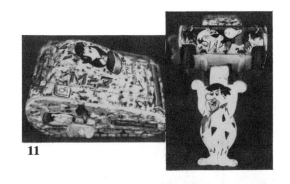

11

12

13

14

15

17

16

18

19

20

21

22

23

24

25

26

27

19
"PEBBLES FLINTSTONE" 9.5x13"
hard cover Big Golden Book with 28-
page story illustrated on every page by
full color art. By Golden Press
© 1963. $35

20
"THE FLINTSTONES" original
comic strip art inked in black on
20x27" white art sheet. Drawn for
1966 Sunday comic strip titled #239
"Air Brakes." $175

21
"THE FLINTSTONES" 10.25x12"
"Sticker Fun" book by Whitman with
four pages of full color punch-out paper stickers plus corresponding pages
with numbered codes for application
of each sticker. By Whitman
© 1961. $65

22
"THE FLINTSTONES" original art
for 1966 Sunday comic strip inked in
black on 20x26" white art sheet. Titled #285 "Nearsighted." $175

23
FLINTSTONES original art for 1967
daily comic strip inked in black on
7.25x22" white sheet. $85

24
"FLINTSTONES" original art for
1967 daily comic strip inked in black
on 7.25x22" white art sheet. $85

25
FLINTSTONES 11.25x22.25" "Great
Big Punchout" book by Whitman
© 1961. Example photo shows front
and back cover. $75

26
"FLINTSTONES COLORING
BOOK" 8.5x11" Whitman
© 1960. $20

27
"WELCOME TO BEDROCK CITY"
2.75" tall tin souvenir cup from Cus-
ter, South Dakota c. 1970. $15

28
FLINTSTONE FAMILY 10 full color
1 ⅜″ full color lithographed tin buttons © 1973. EACH $10

29
''FLINTSTONES TARGET SET'' of
pistol, darts, Flintstone character tin
target in 2x10x12.5″ wide box by
Lido Toys © 1962. Example photo
shows box lid and bottom. $70

30
''FLINTSTONES PLAYSET'' of
''TV-Tinykins'' in 1.5x3.25x6.5″
wide box. By Marx Toys
© 1961. $150

31
''FLINTSTONES PLAYSET'' of
''TV-Tinykins'' in 1.5x3x6.5″ wide
box. By Marx Toys © 1961. $100

32
FLINTSTONES set of six 4.25″ tall
clear glass tumblers issued in 1962 by
Welch's Preserves. Each is lettered in
white with single solid color cartoon
scene. EACH $6

33
''DINO THE DINOSAUR GAME''
by Transogram in 2x8x15″ wide box.
© 1961. $50

34
''HOPPY THE HOPPEROO'' Transogram game © 1964 in 2x8x15″ wide
box. $50

35
''HOW TO CARTOON KIT!'' of art
supplies by Kraftint Corp. © 1981 in
1.5x10x12″ wide box. $50

36
FRED FLINTSTONE pair of 3x5x7″
tall vinyl banks in replica of ''Post
Cocoa Pebbles'' and ''Post Fruity
Pebbles'' cereal boxes © 1984.
EACH $12

28

29

30

31

32

33

34

35

36

Foxy Grandpa

Creator: Charles Edward Schultze

Began: (S) 1/7/1900. New York Herald

Principal Characters: Foxy Grandpa, two unnamed boys.

Synopsis: One of the earliest comic strips with consistent theme of youngsters trying to trick or outwit Foxy with inevitable result of him reversing the attempt against the pranksters. Each strip was signed by Schultze as "Bunny" with a corresponding sketch. A musical comedy of the same name opened in New York City for a two-year duration. The strip ceased circa 1918.

1
FOXY GRANDPA 15x20″ full color newspaper ad poster undated but 1902. $250

2
FOXY GRANDPA 9″ tall diecut, embossed full color valentine by Raphael Tuck © 1906. $100

3
"THE LATEST ADVENTURES OF FOXY GRANDPA" 9.5x15.5″ comic strip book © 1905. $75

4
"FOXY GRANDPA FLIP-FLAPS" 9.5x15.5″ comic strip book © 1905. $75

5
"THE LATEST LARKS OF FOXY GRANDPA" 9.5x15.5″ comic strip book © 1905. $75

6
"THE MERRY PRANKS OF FOXY GRANDPA" 9.5x15.5″ comic strip book © 1905. $75

7
"FOXY GRANDPA'S FROLICS" 9.5x15.5″ comic strip book © 1906. $75

8
"FOXY GRANDPA'S MOTHER GOOSE" 8.5x10″ book c. 1910. $40

9
"FOXY GRANDPA'S MULTIPLIER" 4.5″ diameter mechanical tin disk for learning multiplication tables. Souvenir of 1904 Louisiana Purchase Exposition (St. Louis World's Fair). $100

10
"FOXY GRANDPA RUBBER STAMPS" 5x6″ boxed set from early 1900s. $75

11
"FOXY GRANDPA HAT PARTY"
16x30″ linen picture including 12 hats
to be cut for blindfold party game. c.
1910.   BOXED $150, LOOSE $100,
CUT $50

12
"FOXY GRANDPA'S GROCERY
STORE" 10x14″ cut-out cardboard
supplement sheet from New York
American & Journal newspaper in
1903. $60

13
FOXY GRANDPA 17″ tall stuffed
cloth doll of early 1900s. $100

14
FOXY GRANDPA 5.5″ tall cast iron
bank finished in gold paint. Early
1900s. $100

15
FOXY GRANDPA 5″ tall painted hollow bisque figure with standing Bunny
depicted between legs. Early
1900s. $125

16
FOXY GRANDPA 8.25″ tall painted
hollow bisque figure. Early
1900s. $75

17
FOXY GRANDPA 4.5″ painted and
jointed composition figure. Early
1900s. $100

18
FOXY GRANDPA 3.75″ tall painted
hollow cast iron figure toy with attached iron catapult for tossing tin hat
on figure's head. Early 1900s. $250

19
FOXY GRANDPA 5″ tall German
china cream pitcher c. 1902. $100

20
FOXY GRANDPA 10″ tall painted
composition figure with spring-
mounted nodder head. Early
1900s. $150

21
FOXY GRANDPA 4x4x4″ tall china
head bank c. 1905. $85

22
FOXY GRANDPA & BOYS 6″ long
German-made red clay pipe with
painted character figures. Early
1900s. $85

11

12

13

14

15

16

17

18

19

20

21

22

Gasoline Alley

Creator: Frank King

Began: (S) 11/24/18; (D) 8/23/19. Chicago Tribune-New York News Syndicate.

Principal Characters: Skeezix, Uncle Walt, Auntie Blossom, Corky, Judy, Doc, Uncle Avery, Bill, Nina.

Synopsis: One of the longest-running strips, due partially to the concept of strip characters actually aging from year to year. The featured character, Skeezix Wallet, grew from a foundling infant in 1921 through World War II service to a middle-aged father of the 1960s. Originally intended as an automotive-related strip, it soon became a continuing saga of middle class life.

1

2

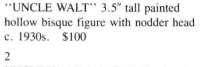
3

4

5

6

7

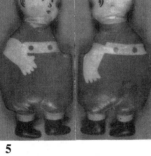
8

9

10

11

1
"UNCLE WALT" 3.5″ tall painted hollow bisque figure with nodder head c. 1930s. $100

2
UNCLE WALT & SKEEZIX painted bisque salt and pepper set with 3.5″ and 2.75″ heights. 1930s.   SET $125

3
"RACHEL" 3.5″ tall painted bisque figure with nodder head. 1930s. $125

4
"SKEEZIX" 2.75″ tall painted bisque figure with nodder head. 1930s. $100

5
"SKEEZIX" 12.5″ tall painted oil-cloth stuffed doll c. 1930s. $50

6
SKEEZIX 6″ tall lithographed tin toothbrush holder marked on chest for "Listerine." 1930s. $125

7
DOG "PAL" 26″ tall animated papier mache store display figure c. 1930s. $300

8
"SKEEZIX PARTY INVITATIONS" in 1x3.5x5.5″ wide box © 1926. $40

9
"GASOLINE ALLEY" Milton Bradley card game in 1x5.5x7.5″ tall box c. 1930s. $40

10
UNCLE WALT "TOOTSIETOY" 2″ long metal car. 1930s. $250

11
"WALT & SKEEZIX" Milton Bradley game in 1x10x18″ wide box. 1930s. $75

12
"SKEEZIX VISITS NINA" Milton
Bradley game in 1x8x14" long box.
1930s. $75

13
"SKEEZIX AND THE AIR MAIL"
Milton Bradley game in 1x8x14" long
box. 1930s. $75

14
"SKEEZIX AND UNCLE WALT"
7.5x9.5" book © 1924. $35

15
"SKEEZIX OUT WEST" 7.5x9.5"
book © 1928. $35

16
"SKEEZIX CRAYON AND COLOR-
ING BOOK" 9x14" © 1933. $35

17
"SKEEZIX DRAWING AND TRAC-
ING BOOK" 9x14" © 1932. $30

18
"SKEEZIX AT THE MILITARY
ACADEMY" Whitman Big Little
Book #1408 © 1938. $30

19
"SKEEZIX ON HIS OWN IN THE
BIG CITY" Whitman All Pictures
Comics Better Little Book #1419
© 1941. $25

20
"SKEEZIX" 8x10" school tablet with
cover art © 1923. $25

21
"SKEEZIX" 8x10" school tablet with
cover art © 1923. $25

22
"PILLSBURY'S COMICOOKY
BAKING SET in 1x5x7" tall box
© 1937. $35

23
"GASOLINE ALLEY" 40x80" three-
sheet poster for 1951 Columbia Pictures film. $100

24
"GASOLINE ALLEY" 5.5" tall
"Sunday Funnies" glass tumbler from
1976 set of eight comic character
glasses. $35

Gene Autry

Creator: Gerald Geraghty (writer), Till Goodan (artist)

Began: (S) 1940; Revived (S) (D) 1952. General Features Syndicate.

Synopsis: Cowboy adventure strip titled originally *Gene Autry Rides*! based on adventures of popular western movie star and radio personality of Gene Autry's Melody Ranch show. The early 1950s revival of the strip was in keeping with the times with added kinds of transportation to supplement his faithful horse Champion. The revival strip ceased in 1955.

1
WRIGLEY GUM 10x12″ cardboard award for merchants c. 1940s. $100

2
AUTRY 8x10″ color Dixie Ice Cream picture c. 1938. $25

3
"PUBLIC COWBOY NO. 1" 8x10″ full color photo c. 1940s. $10

4
"COLUMBIA RECORDS" 8.5x11″ bw photo with record titles on back c. 1940s. $20

5
GENE AUTRY 4x5.5″ laminated color photo plaque c. 1940s. $25

6
"GENE AUTRY IN PUBLIC COWBOY NO. 1" Whitman Big Little Book #1433 © 1938. $25

7
"GENE AUTRY COMICS" #2 Fawcett comic © 1942. $335

8
"GENE AUTRY COWBOY PAINT BOOK" 10x15″ by Merrill Co. © 1940. $35

9
"GENE AUTRY COWBOY ADVENTURES" 10x15″ Merrill Co. coloring book © 1941. $35

10
"GENE AUTRY COLORING BOOK" 11x15″ by Whitman © 1949. $30

11
AUTOGRAPHED "GENE AUTRY COLORING BOOK" 11x15″ by Whitman c. early 1950s. $70

12
"GENE AUTRY CHAMPIONS MAGAZINE" 5.5x8″ retail store premium © 1951. $15

13
GENE AUTRY 14x24″ full color
cover photo from November 5, 1939
supplement to New York Sunday
News. $30

14
"GENE AUTRY'S MELODY
RANCH" 10.5x13″ "Cut-Out Dolls"
book by Whitman c. early
1950s. $90

15
"GENE AUTRY SHOW" 8.5x11″
souvenir program from touring show
c. 1953. $20

16
GENE AUTRY "AIR-WESTERN
ADVENTURE STRIP" 9.5x12.5″
brochure of press publicity materials
by General Features Corp. for introduction of Autry daily strip to pro-
spective newspapers c. late 1952.
Example photo shows brochure cover,
two publicity sheets, detail from one
of the strips. $150

17
"COWBOY SONGS AND MOUN-
TAIN BALLADS" 9x12″ song folio
© 1932 with inside photo of Autry at
WLS (Chicago) radio micro-
phone. $25

18
"COWBOY SONGS AND MOUN-
TAIN BALLADS" 9x12″ "Book No.
2" song folio © 1934. $25

19
"JUKE BOX-RADIO-MOVIE HITS"
9x12″ song folio © 1945. $25

20
"I'M GETTING A MOON'S EYE
VIEW OF THE WORLD" 9x12″
sheet music for song from 12-chapter
1935 movie serial, "The Phantom
Empire," Autry's first starring
role. $15

21
"SOUTH OF THE BORDER
(DOWN MEXICO WAY)" 9x12″
sheet music for title song of 1939
film. $12

13   **14**   **15**

16

17   **18**

19   **20**   **21**

22

23

24

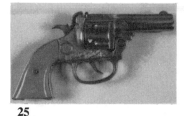

25

26

27

28

29

30

31

22
"GENE AUTRY STENCIL BOOK"
6.5x10″ spiral-bound cardboard album
of western design stencils c. early
1950s. $50

23
"GENE AUTRY ADVENTURE
COMICS" 6.5x8″ "Play-Fun" Pills-
bury premium booklet © 1947. $30

24
"GENE AUTRY" 8″ long silvered
cast iron cap gun with orange plastic
grips by Kenton Toys c. late
1930s. $150

25
"GENE AUTRY" 6″ long snub-nosed
silvered cast iron cap pistol with orange grips by Kenton Toys c. late
1930s. $125

26
"GENE AUTRY" 8″ long silvered
cast iron cap gun with orange plastic
grips by Kenton Toys c. late
1930s. $125

27
GENE AUTRY "RANCH OUTFIT"
cardboard holster and composition gun
set in 2x8x11″ tall box. © 1941 by
M.A. Henry Co. $150

28
"GENE AUTRY" 8″ long silvered
metal cap pistol with white plastic
grips in 1.5x3.5x8″ wide box c.
1940s.   BOXED $175, UNBOXED
$100

29
GENE AUTRY 31″ tall plastic guitar
with carrying case and 16-page song
booklet by Emenee Industries c.
1955.   BOXED $150, UNBOXED
$75

30
"GENE AUTRY" 12″ diameter metal
and cardboard child's drum with
drumsticks and neck cord. c. late
1940s. $75

31
GENE AUTRY metal and leather
spurs in 2x4x7″ wide box c. early
1950s. $75

32
"GENE AUTRY" 3.25" tall metal
pocket flashlight with carrying cord
c. 1950s. $40

33
GENE AUTRY "GOOD LUCK" silvered metal "Horseshoe Nail Ring"
on 3.25x5.25" store card c. 1950.
CARDED $125, RING ONLY $75

34
"GENE AUTRY WESTERN
BRACES" set of elastic suspenders
on 4x8" card c. 1940s. $40

35
"GENE AUTRY" 1¼" bw celluloid
button with pendant ribbons and miniature metal six-shooter c. 1940s. $35

36
"GENE AUTRY" 3.5x4.5" embossed
simulated leather wallet c. 1940s.
$40

37
"GENE AUTRY" 3.5x4.5" plastic
wallet c. 1950s. $40

38
"GENE AUTRY AND CHAMP JR."
child's yellow cotton sweatshirt with
red/black chest art. c. early
1950s. $125

39
GENE AUTRY WRISTWATCH in
silvered metal case engraved on reverse "Always Your Pal-Gene Autry." c. 1948 with original leather
straps. $150

40
"GENE AUTRY/CHAMP" 20" wide
felt pennant inscribed with song title
"Back In The Saddle Again" from
1941 movie. $35

41
"GENE AUTRY" wristwatch with
animated gun hand on dial face that
moves each second. By New Haven
Time Co. c. 1951. $150

42
GENE AUTRY 10x12" full color
photo frame tray inlay jigsaw puzzle
© 1950. $20

43
GENE AUTRY 11x14" full color
photo frame tray inlay jigsaw puzzle
c. early 1950s. $20

32

33

34

35

36

37

38

39

40

41

42
43

The Gumps

Creator: Sidney Smith

Began: (D) 2/12/17; (S) 6/29/19. Chicago Tribune.

Later Artists and/or Writers: Gus Edson (1935).

Principal Characters: Andy Gump, Min Gump, Chester Gump, Tilda the maid, Uncle Bim, Mama De Stross, Ching Chow, Widow Zander.

Synopsis: Long-running humor strip about the foibles of the middle class Gump family and its millionaire relative, Uncle Bim. The strip's popularity in the 1920s-1940s is evidenced by a wealth of related merchandise items and toys. Newspaper publication continued until circa 1960.

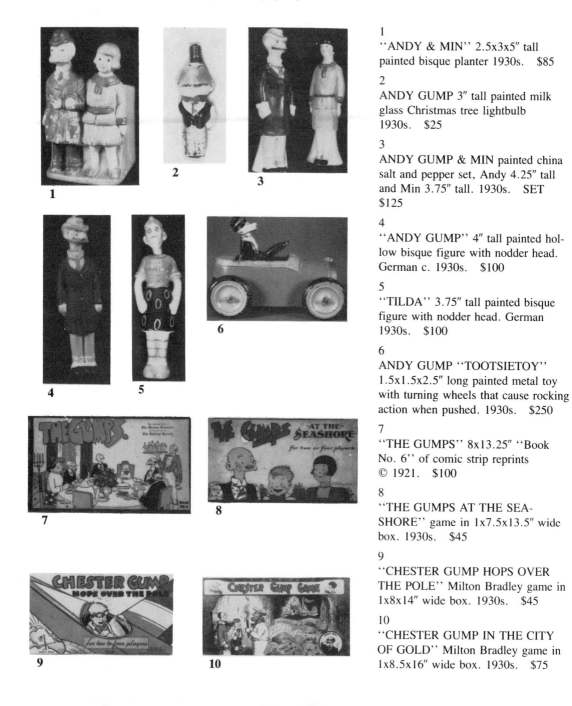

1
"ANDY & MIN" 2.5x3x5" tall painted bisque planter 1930s. $85

2
ANDY GUMP 3" tall painted milk glass Christmas tree lightbulb 1930s. $25

3
ANDY GUMP & MIN painted china salt and pepper set, Andy 4.25" tall and Min 3.75" tall. 1930s.   SET $125

4
"ANDY GUMP" 4" tall painted hollow bisque figure with nodder head. German c. 1930s. $100

5
"TILDA" 3.75" tall painted bisque figure with nodder head. German 1930s. $100

6
ANDY GUMP "TOOTSIETOY" 1.5x1.5x2.5" long painted metal toy with turning wheels that cause rocking action when pushed. 1930s. $250

7
"THE GUMPS" 8x13.25" "Book No. 6" of comic strip reprints © 1921. $100

8
"THE GUMPS AT THE SEA-SHORE" game in 1x7.5x13.5" wide box. 1930s. $45

9
"CHESTER GUMP HOPS OVER THE POLE" Milton Bradley game in 1x8x14" wide box. 1930s. $45

10
"CHESTER GUMP IN THE CITY OF GOLD" Milton Bradley game in 1x8.5x16" wide box. 1930s. $75

11
"ANDY GUMP/HIS LIFE STORY"
5.5x8.5″ book with biography story
© 1924. Example photo shows cover,
title page and its facing page. $25

12
ANDY GUMP 3.25x4.25″ rwb mechanical card published by Philadelphia Public Ledger c. early 1920s.
Example photo shows card in both
mechanical positions plus back
cover. $30

13
"THE GUMPS IN RADIO LAND"
3.5x5.5″ premium storybook by
Gumps radio sponsor Pebeco
© 1937. $35

14
"THE GUMPS" 10x10″ "Book 4"
of comic strip reprints by Cupples &
Leon © 1927. $35

15
"ANDY GUMP FOX TROT" 9x12″
sheet music © 1923. $25

16
"THE GUMPS" 5.75x7″ bridge game
scorepad folder c. 1920s. $20

17
ANDY GUMP "HAPPY NEW
YEAR" 4x5.25″ full color cartoon
greeting card c. 1920s-1930s. $20

18
"CHESTER GUMP FINDS THE
HIDDEN TREASURE" Whitman Big
Little Book #766 © 1934. $30

19
"CHESTER GUMP AND HIS
FRIENDS" 3.5x3.5″ Whitman book
#5 from series obtained as premium
for 12 Tarzan Ice Cream cup lids.
Mid-1930s. $50

20
"CHESTER GUMP FINDS THE
HIDDEN TREASURE" 3.5x6″ Whit-
man book © 1934. $40

Happy Hooligan

Creator: Frederick Burr Opper

Began: (S) 3/25/1900. Hearst Syndicate.

Principal Characters: Happy Hooligan, brother Gloomy Gus, brother Lord Montmorency, dog Flip.

Synopsis: One of several early strips by Opper that continued for more than 30 years although under several title changes. Featured was the well-meaning but ill-fated hobo Hooligan, distinguished throughout his strip life by a tin can hat. Hooligan also appeared in animated silent cartoons, a stage play, sheet music. The newspaper strip ceased in 1932.

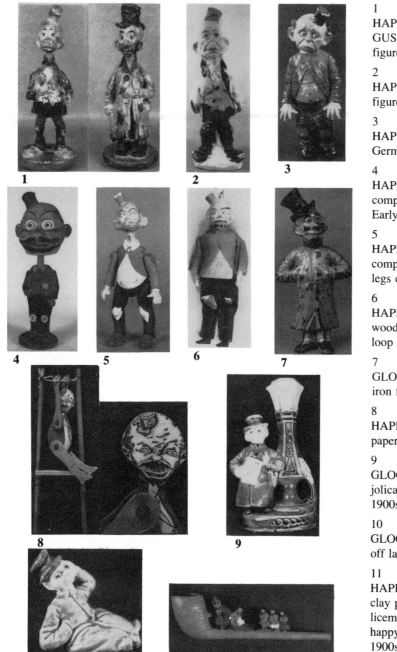

1
HAPPY HOOLIGAN & GLOOMY GUS pair of 11″ tall painted plaster figures c. 1910.   EACH $75

2
HAPPY HOOLIGAN 8.25″ tall bisque figure c. 1910. $50

3
HAPPY HOOLIGAN 5.5″ tall painted German bisque figure c. 1910. $40

4
HAPPY HOOLIGAN 11″ tall painted composition figure with nodder head. Early 1900s. $150

5
HAPPY HOOLIGAN 5″ tall painted composition with movable arms and legs c. 1900s. $100

6
HAPPY HOOLIGAN 9.5″ tall painted wood and composition figure with loop on head c. 1910. $100

7
GLOOMY GUS 5″ tall painted cast iron figure c. 1910. $100

8
HAPPY HOOLIGAN 8″ tall wood and paper trapeze toy c. 1910. $50

9
GLOOMY GUS 2.5x3.5x7″ tall Majolica china candleholder. Early 1900s. $100

10
GLOOMY GUS 2.5″ tall china figure off larger piece c. 1910. $35

11
HAPPY HOOLIGAN 5.5″ long red clay pipe showing him pulled by policeman to police station as three unhappy Hooligan toddlers watch. Early 1900s. $85

12
HAPPY HOOLIGAN 5.5″ tall glazed ceramic bank c. 1910. $60

13
HAPPY HOOLIGAN 3x3x2.5″ tall unpainted white bisque over fired red clay paperweight c. 1910. $50

14
HAPPY 14″ tall valentine by Raphael Tuck 1905. $75

15
"HAPPY HOOLIGAN AND HIS BROTHER GLOOMY GUS" 10x14″ comic strip reprint book by New York American & Journal © 1902. $100

16
"HAPPY HOOLIGAN" 10x14″ comic strip reprint book by New York American & Journal © 1903. $100

17
HAPPY 10x13″ book by McLoughlin Brothers © 1932. $60

18
HOOLIGAN characters cardboard targets with wood bases c. 1925. Adults are 8.5″ tall and kids are 4.5″ tall. EACH FIGURE $12

19
"HAPPY HOOLIGAN" 5x9″ school tablet from "The Funnies" series © 1928. $30

20
HAPPY HOOLIGAN on 9.5x12″ cardboard with pencil and black ink sketch signed by Opper January 18, 1926. $150

21
"HAPPY HOOLIGAN CHARACTERISTIC DANCE AND TWO-STEP" 10.5x13″ sheet music with Opper photo. © 1902. $50

22
"HAPPY HOOLIGAN'S RECEPTION" 11x13″ sheet music supplement from Oct. 19, 1902 New York American & Journal. $35

23
"HAPPY HOOLIGAN'S THANKSGIVING TURKEY" 3.5x5.5″ mechanical postcard © 1906. $20

24
HAPPY HOOLIGAN 3.5x5.5″ New Year card. © 1906. $20

12   **13**   **14**

15   **16**

17   **18**   **19**

20   **21**   **22**

23   **24**

Harold Teen

Creator: Carl Ed

Began: (S) 5/4/19 (Chicago Tribune); (D) 9/25/19 (New York Daily News).

Principal Characters: Harold Teen, Lillums, Shadow, Pop Jenks, Beezie, Horace, Goofy.

Synopsis: Probably the earliest strip devoted to teenage life and certainly well-accepted by teen readers for the next two decades. The strip served as a changing lexicon for new teen terms and fads, centered in Pop Jenks' Sugar Bowl soda fountain parlor. Movie versions were released in 1928 and 1933. The newspaper strip ceased in 1959 with Ed's death.

1
"HAROLD TEEN" & "LILLUMS" 3.75″ tall painted bisque figures. 1930s.   EACH $35

2
"POP JENKS" 3.75″ tall painted German bisque figure with nodder head. 1930s. $90

3
"LILLUMS" 3.5″ painted German bisque figure with nodder head. 1930s. $90

4
"THE ADVENTURES OF HAROLD TEEN" 7x8.5″ Cupples & Leon comic strip book © 1931. $75

5
"HAROLD TEEN COLOR AND PAINT BOOK" 9.5x13″ by McLoughlin Brothers © 1932. $40

6
"HAROLD TEEN" 2.5x2.75″ full color strip card from set of eight published in 1930s larger set of comic character strip cards.   EACH CARD $8

7
"HAROLD TEEN GAME" by Milton Bradley in 2x8x14″ wide box. 1930s. $50

8
"COMIC BAT-O-BALL" 9.5″ tall cardboard paddles, each with attached rubber string and ball. Pictured are Shadow, Lillums, Harold Teen. Morton's Salt premiums © 1938.   EACH $25

9
"HAROLD TEEN UKE" 20″ tall pressed wood ukulele with generic carrying case. 1930s. $200

Henry

Creator: Carl Anderson

Began: (D) 12/17/34; (S) 3/10/35. King Features Syndicate.

Later Artists and/or Writers: John Liney, Don Trachte, Jack Tippet, Dick Hodgins

Principal Characters: Henry, look-alike girlfriend Henrietta.

Synopsis: Strip based on weekly magazine cartoon begun in 1932 featuring bald-headed, mute youngster with never-changing facial expression. Other characters appearing in the strip are also mute, and adventure is conveyed entirely in pantomime art. The strip still continued into the early 1990s.

1
"HENRY" 6.75" tall painted bisque figure with movable arms.
© 1934. $175

2
"HENRY" 8" tall painted hard rubber doll with movable arms.
© 1934. $100

3
HENRY & LITTLE BROTHER 7" tall celluloid wind-up toy connected by ribbon to smaller figure also on wheeled platform. 1930s. $300

4
"HENRY ON ELEPHANT" 3x6" tall by 8" long celluloid wind-up toy in original box. 1930s. BOXED $800, LOOSE $500

5
HENRY set of four 2.5" tall diecut celluloid name card holders on base. 1930s. EACH $40

6
"HENRY" 10x10" Book No. 1 of comic strip reprints by David McKay Co. © 1935. $75

7
"HENRY" 5.5x7" comic strip reprint book by David McKay Co.
© 1945. $30

8
"HENRY PAINT BOOK" 8x11" by Whitman © 1951. $20

9
"HENRY GOES TO A PARTY" 6.25x8" Wonder Book #1508 © 1955 with lightly embossed cover art and spiral binding. $15

10
"HENRY IN LOLLIPOP LAND" 6.25x8" Wonder Book © 1953. $15

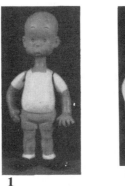

1

2

3

4

5

6

7

8

9

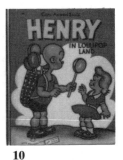

10

Hopalong Cassidy

Creator: William Boyd, Dan Spiegle (artist)

Began: (D) (S) 1949. Los Angeles Mirror Syndicate.

Principal Characters: Hopalong Cassidy (William Boyd), Topper (his horse), Mesquite Jenkins.

Synopsis: Western adventure strip featuring extremely popular cowboy superstar of the early 1950s television era following several years of comic book appearances and many earlier films. The original Hopalong Cassidy character was created by Clarence E. Mulford circa 1907. The newspaper strip continued into 1955.

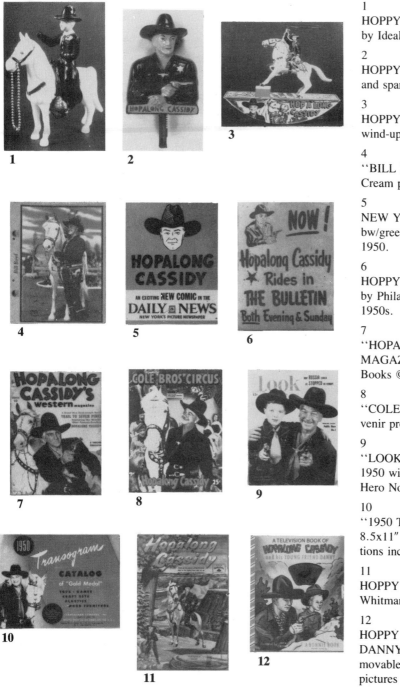

1

HOPPY ON TOPPER 6″ tall plastic by Ideal Toy c. 1950. $125

2

HOPPY 3.5″ tall plastic noisemaker and sparkler c. 1950. $100

3

HOPPY 2x7″ tall by 7.5″ long tin wind-up by Marx c. 1950. $350

4

"BILL BOYD" 8x10″ Dixie Ice Cream premium c. 1940s. $40

5

NEW YORK DAILY NEWS 10x13″ bw/green cardboard poster. 1950. $200

6

HOPPY 15x20″ rw cardboard poster by Philadelphia Bulletin early 1950s. $150

7

"HOPALONG CASSIDY WESTERN MAGAZINE" Vol. 1 #2 by Best Books © 1951. $75

8

"COLE BROS. CIRCUS" 9x12″ souvenir program 1950. $50

9

"LOOK" magazine for Aug. 29, 1950 with cover article about "Public Hero No. 1." $20

10

"1950 TRANSOGRAM CATALOG" 8.5x11″ with 40 pages of toy illustrations including 11 Hoppy items. $125

11

HOPPY 11x14″ punch-out book by Whitman © 1951. $150

12

HOPPY & "YOUNG FRIEND DANNY" 6x8″ Bonnie Book with movable wheel to create "television" pictures c. 1950. $35

13
HOPPY 8x10″ school tablet with spiral binding. 1950. $50

14
HOPPY "WRITING PAPER WITH ENVELOPES" in 8x11″ cardboard holder. By Whitman © 1950. $75

15
HOPPY 6x11.5″ paper wall calendar for 1952 with different Hoppy photo portrait for each month. $200

16
"HOPALONG CASSIDY BICYCLES" 12x18″ bwr paper poster for bicycle awards by local theater in early 1950s. $200

17
"BOND BREAD" 21x27″ bwbl cardboard poster. 1950. $100

18
"BOND BREAD" 3x5.5″ full color premium card. 1950. $25

19
"BOND BREAD" 9x15″ "Hang-Up Album" for set of 16 bread loaf end labels. 1950. $150

20
"BOND BREAD" 5.5x8.5″ bw handbill for bread labels. 1950. $35

21
"BOND BREAD" 5.5x8.5″ bw handbill for bread labels. 1950. $35

22
HOPPY AUTOGRAPHED card 5x7″ from recognition dinner for him in Philadelphia Nov. 26, 1952. $150

23
"HOPALONG CASSIDY WESTERN SERIES" of seven 2.25″ tall painted metal figures of Hoppy and six cowboys in 15″ wide box. By Timpo of England c. 1950. $350

24
"HOPALONG CASSIDY WRIST-WATCH" in bwr 4x7″ box. 1950. BOXED $400, LOOSE $50

25
"HOPALONG CASSIDY WRIST-WATCH" in 3x4x4″ tall box. 1950. BOXED $300, LOOSE $50

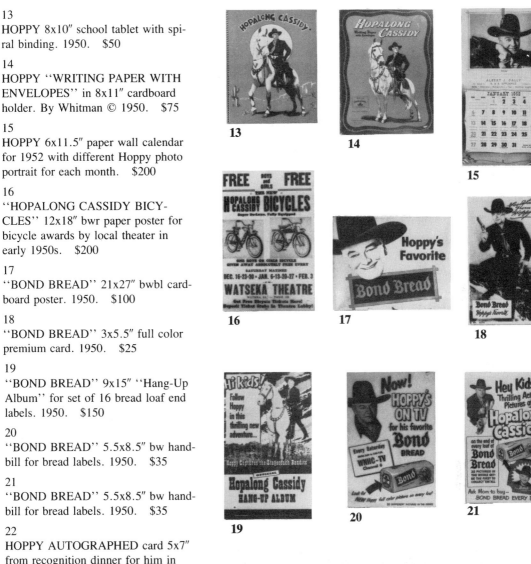

13   14   15   16   17   18   19   20   21   22   23   24   25

26

27

28

29

30

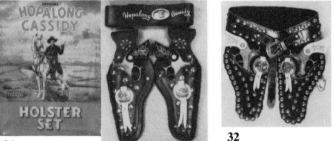

31

32

33

34

35

36

37

26
"HOPALONG CASSIDY" 5.5" tall black metal alarm clock by US Time Corp. c. 1950. $300

27
"HOPALONG CASSIDY COOKIE BARREL" 6.5" diameter by 11" tall ceramic jar c. 1950. $350

28
"HOPALONG CASSIDY" 3x3x4" tall black plastic camera with aluminum front. 1950s. $125

29
"HOPALONG CASSIDY" 5x5x9" wide Arvin radio with silver/black foil design on front c. 1950. $300

30
"WESTERN FRONTIER SET" of eight sheets of full color punch-outs to form 3-D figures. By Milton Bradley © 1950 in 1x13x19" wide box. $250

31
"HOPALONG CASSIDY HOLSTER SET" of cap guns and holsters in 3x9x14" tall box c. 1950. BOXED $700, LOOSE $500

32
"HOPALONG CASSIDY" double cap gun and holster set featuring 8.5" long silvered metal guns with ivory plastic grips picturing him on both sides. c. 1950. $500

33
HOPPY "4 TELEVISION PUZZLES" in 2x12x12" box with lid art image of television set c. 1950. $125

34
"5-PIECE GYM" set of rubber physical developement toys in 2x12x16" wide box c. 1950. $300

35
HOPPY 16x26" full color lithographed tin target by Marx c. 1950. $150

36
HOPPY 9.5x16x23" tall tin laundry hamper c. 1950s. $200

37
"HOPALONG CASSIDY'S POPCORN" 5" tall lithographed tin canister c. 1950. SEALED $125, OPENED $90

38
HOPPY "AND THE SINGING BANDIT" 12x12" Capitol Records album containing records and related illustrated story script. © 1950. $50

39
HOPALONG CASSIDY "WESTERN STYLE DOMINOES" set by Milton Bradley in 2x9.5x12" wide box. © 1950. $100

40
HOPPY "WOODBURNING SET" in 3x13x17" wide box. c. 1950. $150

41
HOPPY "BAR-20 SCHOOL SLATE OUTFIT" of school supplies by Transogram © 1950 in 3x13x17" wide box. $85

42
HOPPY child's pair of bw leather boots in 4x7x10" tall box. Boots are by Acme Co. © 1951. BOXED $300, LOOSE $150

43
HOPPY 3.5x4.5" black leather wallet with front panel of gold colored metal that has full color decal. c. 1950. $100

44
"HOPALONG CASSIDY" 7x9x4" deep flat steel lunch box by Aladdin Industries © 1954. $250

45
"HOPALONG CASSIDY" 12x19" full color vinyl placemat c. 1950. $100

46
HOPPY "BAR-20 TV CHAIR" 12x12x24" tall wood folding chair c. 1950. $300

47
"HOPALONG CASSIDY PENCIL CASE" 2x5x11" wide rigid cardboard with contents including paper portrait fold-out sheet. c. 1950. $85

48
"HOPALONG CASSIDY" 36x72" chenille throw rug c. 1950. $75

38   **39**

40

41

42   **43**

44   **45**

46

47

48

Howdy Doody

Creator: Chad Grothkopf, copyright by Bob Smith.

Began: 1950

Other Artists and/or Writers: Milt Neil, Edward Kean, Stan Lee.

Principal Characters: Howdy Doody, Buffalo Bob, Clarabell, Mr. Bluster, Princess Summerfall Winterspring, Dilly Dally, Flub-A-Dub, numerous other occasional characters.

Synopsis: Sunday strip based on the first popular children's television show introduced in 1947 by former radio show *Triple B Ranch* host Bob Smith. The TV version, originally titled *Puppet Playhouse,* involved marionette antics presided over by living characters Buffalo Bob (Smith) and clown Clarabell Hornblow in either the Club House of Doodyville or the slightly later circus setting. The comic strip did not achieve the immense popularity of the television version and ceased in 1953. The TV series ran until the late 1950s and was briefly revived by NBC-TV in 1976.

1

2

3

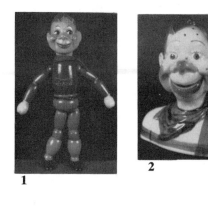

5

6

4

4

8

7

9

1
"HOWDY DOODY" 12.5″ tall jointed wood doll with composition head. Name decal has Bob Smith copyright c. 1950. $350

2
HOWDY DOODY 4x7x9″ tall ceramic bust portrait bank c. early 1950s. $300

3
HOWDY DOODY 2.5″ tall hard white plastic figurine by Marx Toys © Kagran c. 1951-1956. $60

4
HOWDY DOODY 20″ tall cloth doll with plastic head by Ideal Toys c. early 1950s. $200

5
HOWDY "THE PIN THAT TALKS" plastic head with talking tape on 4x5.5″ card © Kagran c. 1951-1956. $75

6
"HOWDY DOODY MARIONETTE" 15″ tall wood and composition with fabric outfit in original box c. 1952. BOXED $175, LOOSE $100

7
PRINCESS 13″ tall marionette of wood composition with fabric outfit c. 1952. $135

8
FLUB-A-DUB 12″ long marionette of wood with composition head and fabric outfit c. 1952. $250

9
FLUB-A-DUB   7″ tall composition puppet with vinyl head and fabric outfit c. 1952. $100

10
"HOWDY DOODY PHONO DOO-
DLE" 10x10x7" tall record player
c. early 1950s. $200

11
HOWDY DOODY 5.5" tall painted
hard plastic electrical lamp base figure
on 5.5" diameter wood base. Early
1950s. $65

12
HOWDY & SANTA 10x14" thin
molded plastic wall lamp © Kagran
c. 1951-1956. $150

13
"TV DIGEST" 5.5x8.5" issue for
week of November 17, 1951 with
Howdy cover article. $40

14
HOWDY "POLL-PARROT'S
PHOTO ALBUM" 8.5x11" premium
photo book © Bob Smith c. 1948-
1951. COMPLETE $125, NO PIC-
TURES $60

15
"JACK AND JILL" 7x10" issue of
child's magazine for January 1960
with Howdy cover article. $10

16
HOWDY DOODY 3" tall red plastic
mug with full color decal. Ovaltine
premium © Bob Smith c. 1948-
1951. $35

17
HOWDY DOODY 5" tall blue plastic
shake-up mug with full color decal.
Ovaltine premium © Bob Smith
c. 1948-1951. $50

18
"HOWDY DOODY PAINT SET" by
Milton Bradley in 2x9x12" wide box
c. early 1950s. $60

19
HOWDY set of five 4" tall plastic mechanical puppet figure toys on 6x8"
card c. early 1950s. $75

20
"HOWDY DOODY" 17x18x25" tall
vinyl and wood child's platform rocking chair c. early 1950s. $200

21
"HOWDY DOODY" 12x15x23" tall
canvas and aluminum folding chair
c. early 1950s. $125

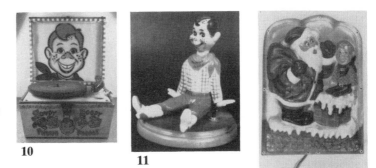
10 **11**

12

13

14

15

16

17

18 **19**

20

21

Jack Armstrong

Creator: Bob Schoenke

Began: 1947. Register & Tribune Syndicate.

Principal Characters: Jack Armstrong, detective Vic Hardy.

Synopsis: Short-lived newspaper strip based on the fading popularity of "The All American Boy" who enjoyed tremendous radio popularity under sponsorship of Wheaties from the mid-1930s into the World War II years. The early period accounted for nearly all of the many Jack Armstrong premium items. The newspaper strip ceased in 1949.

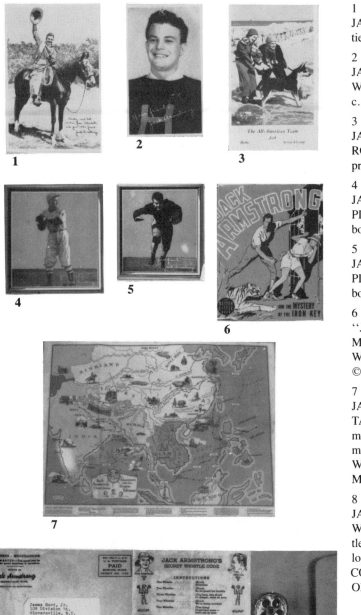

1
JACK ARMSTRONG 5x8″ bw Wheaties premium photo c. 1933. $20

2
JACK ARMSTRONG 3x5.5″ bw Wheaties premium photo c. 1934. $15

3
JACK ARMSTRONG/BETTY/ARROW CHAMP 3x5.5″ bw Wheaties premium photo c. 1934. $15

4
JACK ARMSTRONG/BASEBALL PLAYER 6x6.5″ blw/orange Wheaties box back panel c. 1934. $20

5
JACK ARMSTRONG/FOOTBALL PLAYER 6x6.5″ blw/orange Wheaties box back panel c. 1935. $20

6
"JACK ARMSTRONG AND THE MYSTERY OF THE IRON KEY" Whitman Better Little Book #1432 © 1939. $30

7
JACK ARMSTRONG "DRAGON TALISMAN" 20x27″ Wheaties premium map game c. 1936 in 7x10.5″ mailing envelope.   COMPLETE WITH PLAYING PIECES $250, MAP ONLY $150

8
JACK ARMSTRONG "EGYPTIAN WHISTLE RING" with Secret Whistle Code sheet in 4x6.5″ mailing envelope. Wheaties premium c. 1938. COMPLETE $100, RING ONLY $50

9

"BIG TEN" FOOTBALL GAME
Wheaties premium c. 1936. $40

9

10

TORPEDO FLASHLIGHTS each a
4.5″ long 1939 Wheaties premium in
red, blue or black cardboard. EACH
$15

11

"SECRET BOMBSIGHT"
1x2.5x3.5″ long wood and paper toy
with three wood bombs and paper ship
targets. Wheaties premium c. 1942.
WITH ALL BOMBS $150, WITH
UNCUT SHEET $200

10 **11**

12

"JACK ARMSTRONG IN AFRICA"
plastic/metal viewer with bw 35mm
filmstrip. Wheaties premium
c. 1937. COMPLETE $100, UN-
BOXED $75

13

"PARACHUTE BALL" set of aluminum ball, fabric parachute and instruction sheet. Wheaties premium
c. 1946. COMPLETE $125, UN-
BOXED $75

12 **13**

14

"MAGIC ANSWER BOX" 3.75″ tall
red lithographed tin Wheaties premium c. 1940. COMPLETE $100,
UNBOXED $75

15

"BREAKFAST OF CHAMPIONS"
5″ diameter glass cereal bowl Wheaties premium c. 1937. $50

14

16

"SQUADRON NC 38" cardboard
and aluminum toy airplane 8.5″ long.
Wheaties premium c. 1940. $150

17

WHEATIES 1944 premium "Tru-Flite
Model Warplane Series" of unpunched color sheets for assembly of
two aircraft with instruction sheet in
7x10″ mailing envelope. Seven sets
offered. EACH $75

15 **16**

18

JACK ARMSTRONG individual plane
with instruction sheet, see item
17. UNPUNCHED, EACH $30

17 **18**

Joe Palooka

Creator: Ham Fisher

Began: 1928, Syndicated 1/1/31. New York Mirror.

Later Artists and/or Writers: Moe Leff, Joe Certa, Tony DiPreta, Morris Weiss.

Principal Characters: Joe Palooka, manager Knobby Walsh, girlfriend and later wife Ann Howe, buddy Jerry Leemy, valet Smokey, Humphrey Pennyworth, Little Max.

Synopsis: One of the few sports strips, and the first devoted exclusively to boxing. Palooka, the epitome of morality, virtue and many other ideals to countless readers, continued defending his heavyweight championship for over half a century. His marriage to Ann Howe in 1949 was one of the most widely-known social events in newspaper strip history. Publication ceased in 1984.

1

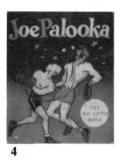

7

8

1
JOE PALOOKA 3x5″ ''School Bus Safety Tips'' comic booklet © 1950. $20

2
''JOE PALOOKA'' 4″ tall jointed and painted wood figure with stamped name on chest. c. 1930s. $150

3
''JOE PALOOKA'' ORIGINAL ART by Ham Fisher inked in black on white 17x23″ sheet for undated but 1940s Sunday newspaper comic strip. $200

4
''JOE PALOOKA'' Whitman Big Little Book #1123 © 1934. $30

5
''GENTLEMAN JOE PALOOKA'' Saalfield book #1176 in Big Little Book format © 1940. $25

6
''JOE PALOOKA'S GREAT ADVENTURE'' Saalfield Book #1168 in Big Little Book format undated c. 1940s. $25

7
''JOAN PALOOKA'' vinyl and fabric Palooka daughter hand puppet with birth certificate in 4x8x12″ tall box. © 1952.   BOXED $75, UNBOXED $35

8
''LITTLE MAX'S LUNCH'' 2.5x3x4.25″ tall pink plastic figural bank and candy container in box c. late 1940s.   BOXED $65, UNBOXED $30

9
JOE PALOOKA "HI THERE!" 5x6″ comic booklet with 20 pages for American Red Cross © 1949. $10

10
JOE PALOOKA "WORLD CHAMP" 8″ long tan leather-like football with white plastic lacing c. 1940s. $35

11
"JOE PALOOKA" wristwatch © 1947 by New Haven Time Co. $300

12
JOE PALOOKA 3.5x5″ bw portrait card c. 1940s. $15

13
"JOE PALOOKA" rwb/fleshtone cardboard box in original flattened 3.25x7″ size. From boxed candy, toy and card series by Comics Novelty Candy Corp. c. 1940s. $65

14
JOE PALOOKA "BOP BAG" inflatible vinyl punching bag with raised image of Palooka's boxing gloves that squeak when struck. By Ideal Toys © 1952 in 6x7x7″ tall rwb box. $75

15
JOE PALOOKA "PUNCHIN' BAG" 8.5″ steel and lithographed paper inflation pump for vinyl boxing toy by Dodger Sporting Goods Corp. c. late 1940s. $30

16
JOE PALOOKA "BASKETBALL SET" of child's basketball and inflation pump in 12x12x12″ box. c. 1940s. $45

17
JOE PALOOKA "BOXING GAME" featuring boxing ring playing board. By Lowell Toys c. 1950s in 2x12x16″ wide box. $75

18
"JOE PALOOKA LUNCH KIT" 4x5x7″ long lithographed steel lunch box with full color art on all panels. © 1948. $125

9

10

11

12

13

14   **15**

16

17

18

The Katzenjammer Kids

Creator: Rudolph Dirks

Began: 12/12/1897. New York Journal.

Later Artists and/or Writers: Harold Knerr, Doc Winner, Joe Musial, Hy Eisman, others.

Principal Characters: Hans, Fritz, Mamma, der Captain, der Inspector, Rollo Rhubarb, Lena, Miss Twiddle.

Synopsis: Generally acknowledged as the first continuity newpaper comic strip, although patterned after the 19th century German cartoon feature *Max und Moritz* by Wilhelm Busch. The title was changed briefly in the Dirks era to *The Captain and the Kids* due to a publishing contract legal battle. Another title change to *The Shenanigan Kids* occurred between 1918-1920 due to World War I anti-German sentiment.

1

2

3

4

5

6   **7**   **8**

1
RUDOLPH DIRKS original art and signature from 1960 in black ink on 2.75x4″ paper sheet. $125

2
MAMMA & KIDS 2x4x5″ tall painted hollow bisque figure c. 1920s. $175

3
MAMMA & KIDS 1.5x3.5x4.5″ tall painted hollow celluloid figure with head of each kid jointed by elastic stringing. c. 1930s. $200

4
MAMMA 6″ tall painted German bisque figure c. 1920s. $100

5
MAMMA 2.5x2.5x3″ wide pottery china head bank made in Austria c. 1910. $100

6
"THE CAPT." 4.5″ tall painted composition wood figure © 1944. $100

7
"HANS" 2.75″ tall painted composition wood figure © 1944. $85

8
"FRITZ" 2.75″ tall painted composition wood figure © 1944. $85

9
KATZENJAMMER set of hollow rubber figures © 1938 by Schavoir Rubber Co. Captain 6.5″ tall and Kids are 5″ tall. SET $250

10
KATZENJAMMER 3.5x5.5″ full color Christmas postcard © 1906. $15

11
KATZENJAMMER 9″ tall full color diecut and jointed valentine by Raphael Tuck © 1906. $85

12
MUSIC FOLIO 9x12″ ''Song Hits From The Great Cartoon Hit Musical Comedy'' © 1920. $30

13
''THE KATZENJAMMER KIDS'' 4x5.5″ Dell Fast-Action Book #14 © 1942. $50

14
''IN THE MOUNTAINS'' 3.5x8″ Saalfield book © 1934. $60

15
''HANS AND FRITZ'' 10x14″ comic strip book by Saalfield © 1917. $50

16
''THE KATZENJAMMER KIDS'' 8x8″ spiral-bound book with animated story art moved by wheels and tabs. © 1945. $40

17
''KATZENJAMMER KIDS'' 8.5x11″ Whitman book © 1937. $50

18
CAPTAIN 1 ⅛″ lithographed tin pinback button from 1930s newspaper series. $25

19
''FUNNY PAGE JIG-SAW PUZZLE'' in 1x6.25x9.25″ wide box. Puzzle is 10x14″ with full color comic strip. By Transogram © 1938. $35

20
''THE CAPTAIN AND THE KIDS'' Milton Bradley game © 1947 in 1x9x15″ wide box. $35

21
''KATZENJAMMER KIDS HOCKEY'' Jaymar game c. late 1940s in 1x7x10″ wide box. Photo shows lid and board. $30

9

10

11

12

13

14

15

16

17

18

19

20

21

The Kewpies

Creator: Rose O'Neill

Began: (S) 1935. Hearst Syndicate.

Synopsis: A late entry and short-lived Sunday newspaper strip was based on the popularity of Kewpies who were first established prior to 1910. The newspaper version continued the popular image of Kewpies as elfin-like cherubs in charming activities almost entirely devoid of human characteristics. The newspaper strip ceased in 1937 although Kewpie popularity continues to the present.

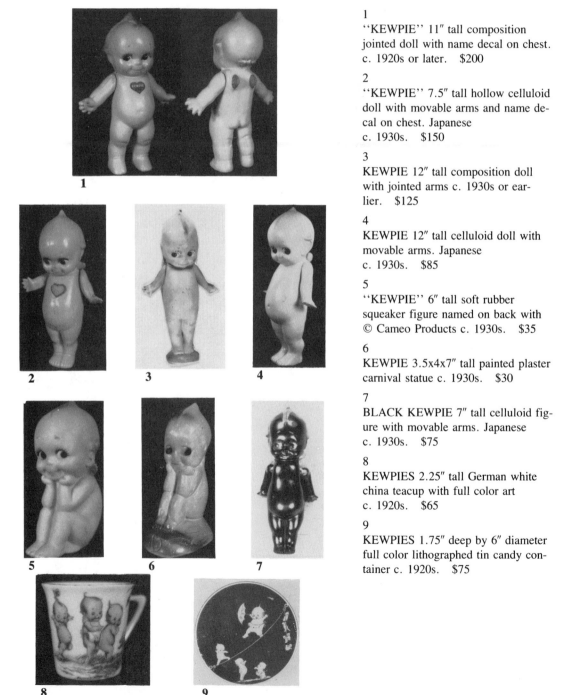

1

2   3   4

5   6   7

8   9

1
''KEWPIE'' 11″ tall composition jointed doll with name decal on chest. c. 1920s or later. $200

2
''KEWPIE'' 7.5″ tall hollow celluloid doll with movable arms and name decal on chest. Japanese c. 1930s. $150

3
KEWPIE 12″ tall composition doll with jointed arms c. 1930s or earlier. $125

4
KEWPIE 12″ tall celluloid doll with movable arms. Japanese c. 1930s. $85

5
''KEWPIE'' 6″ tall soft rubber squeaker figure named on back with © Cameo Products c. 1930s. $35

6
KEWPIE 3.5x4x7″ tall painted plaster carnival statue c. 1930s. $30

7
BLACK KEWPIE 7″ tall celluloid figure with movable arms. Japanese c. 1930s. $75

8
KEWPIES 2.25″ tall German white china teacup with full color art c. 1920s. $65

9
KEWPIES 1.75″ deep by 6″ diameter full color lithographed tin candy container c. 1920s. $75

TOOTHBRUSH HOLDERS (All are c. 1930s and each is marked "Japan" except The Lone Ranger. Each is 4–5" tall)

"Uncle Walt" glazed ceramic. **$75** "Skippy" bisque with movable arm. **$50** "Minnie Mouse" bisque with movable arm. **$200** "Mickey Mouse" bisque with movable arm. **$200** "Orphan Annie" glazed ceramic. **$125** Donald Duck bisque for two brushes. **$250** "Moon Mullins" glazed ceramic. **$75** "Kayo" glazed ceramic. **$75** "Uncle Willie" glazed ceramic. **$75** Henry and Henrietta bisque for two brushes. **$250** "Popeye" bisque with pipe and movable arm. **$175** "Andy & Min" (Gump) bisque. **$85** "Uncle Walt & Skeezix" bisque. **$85** "Moon Mullins & Kayo" bisque. **$85** "The Lone Ranger" wood composition. **$65** Little Orphan Annie and Sandy bisque for two brushes. **$150**

GAMES

"Popeye Ring Toss" lithographed tin by Durable Toy and Novelty Corp., 1935. **$250** "Donald Duck's Party Game for Young Folks" by Parker Brothers, 1938. **$100** "The Flintstones Big Game Hunt" by Whitman, 1962. **$75** "Hopalong Cassidy Game" by Milton Bradley, 1950. **$85** "Batman and Robin Game" by Hasbro, 1965. **$50** "The Game of Li'l Abner" by Milton Bradley, 1944. **$65** "Buck Rogers Game of the 25th Century A.D." by Stephen Slesinger, Inc., 1934. **$250** "Gene Autry's Dude Ranch Game" by Built-Rite, 1956. **$75** "Dick Tracy Super Detective Mystery Card Game" by Whitman, 1941. **$50**

"Disneyland" Belgium-made for use in Great Britain, probably as a biscuit container, c. 1939. **$500** "Buster Brown Cigar" with R.F. Outcault artist's signature, c. 1926. Missing lid, **$800;** complete, **$1,200** "Hopalong Cassidy's Favorite Pop Corn," c. 1950. Opened, **$90;** sealed, **$125** "Howdy Doody Official Outdoor Sports Box" by Liberty Steel Chest Corp., c. 1956. **$150** "Comic Candies" by Candy Corporation of America, depicting seven look-alike characters, c. 1940s. **$50** "Yellow Kid" sand pail © 1896 by R. F. Outcault. **$1,500** Donald painting Mickey, food product container from Great Britain, c. 1939. **$250** Donald, Minnie and Mickey triangular food product containers used in Australia and possibly other British Commonwealth nations, c. 1936. Each, **$300** "Mickey Mouse Fishing Kit" by Hamilton Metal Products Co., 1935–36. **$500**

NEWSPAPER COMIC STRIP PROMOTIONAL BUTTONS   (Most are 1¼″ diameter, others to the same scale)

Andy Gump "Follow the Gumps in The News Leader," 1930s. **$40** Buster Brown and Tige "New York Herald/Young Folks," c. 1905.
$200 Dick Tracy with back paper "Read Dick Tracy Every Day in The Chicago Tribune," 1930s. **$50** Dick Tracy with back paper "Read
Dick Tracy Every Day in the News/New York's Picture Newspaper," 1930s. **$50** "Flash Gordon Club/Chicago Herald and Examiner,"
1930s. **$150** " 'Foxy Grandpa' Presented by The New York Journal," c. 1900. **$75** "Ignatz Mouse/New York Evening Journal" from
series of contest buttons, 1930s. **$35** Jiggs/"Examiner/L.A. Playground Contest," 1930s. **$50** Joe Palooka "Sunday Bulletin/Tangle
Comics," c. 1950s. **$35** "Just Kids Safety Club/Chicago American" showing Marjory, 1930s. **$25** Li'l Abner "Sunday Bulletin/Tangle
Comics," c. 1950s. **$35** Mickey Mouse "30 Comics/Sunday Herald and Examiner," 1930s. **$125** Mickey Mouse "1979 Disney World
Winner!/The Detroit News," 1979. **$35** Mutt & Jeff "Join The Evening Telegraph 'Mutt & Jeff' Club," c. 1915. **$50** "The Phantom's
Club/Member," Australian issue, c. 1960s. **$250** Popeye "Member Comic Club/S.F. Examiner," 1930s. **$40** "Reg'lar Fellers Legion of
Honor," issuer unknown, 1930s. **$40** "Tailspin Tommy Club Member/The Evening Sun," 1930s. **$75** "Wonder Woman/Sensation
Comics," comic book premium, c. 1942. **$250** Superman, Nancy, Sluggo and Parrot "Sun-Times Comic Capers Club," 1940s.
$350 Multi-character "21 Comics In Color/Sunday Detroit Times," 1930s. **$40** "Howdy Doody/New Color Comic - Sunday's News,"

PHILADELPHIA "EVENING LEDGER COMICS" BUTTON SET   (Each is 1¼" diameter; 1930s)

"Ledger Fun Club" pictures Relentless Rudolph with a back paper advertising the comic section of the "Sunday Public Ledger." **$100**. The following come with back papers inscribed "Listen To Brother Bill/Every Day 6 P.M./WIP" (radio station) or "World's Most Famous Comics/Evening Ledger Every Day": Relentless Rudolph, **$75**; Mickey Mouse, **$250**; Minnie Mouse, **$250**; Smitty, **$75**; Snuffy Smith, **$100**; Babe Bunting, **$50**; Bobby Thatcher, **$50**; Dan Dunn, **$75**; Popeye, **$150**; Harold Teen, **$75**; Connie, **$50**; Wimpy, **$150**; Felix, **$200**.

NEWSPAPER COWBOY COMIC STRIP PROMOTIONAL BUTTONS   (Same scale as above. Hopalong Cassidy, all c. 1950; Red Ryder, c. late 1940s; The Lone Ranger, c. late 1930s)

Hopalong Cassidy/Chicago Tribune. **$35** Hopalong Cassidy/The Detroit News. **$75** Hopalong Cassidy/Daily News. **$50** Hopalong Cassidy/Sun-Tele. **$75** Red Ryder/Pony Contest. **$20** Hopalong Cassidy/Toronto Star. **$150** Hopalong Cassidy/The Journal. **$100** The Lone Ranger/Sunday Herald and Examiner. **$25** Lone Ranger/Reading Times. **$75**

KELLOGG'S PEP CEREAL BUTTON SET

Pictured is the complete set of 86 lithographed tin buttons. Each is $^{13}/_{16}$" diameter, made of lithographed tin with ''Kellogg's Pep'' printed on the reverse in blue on silver. Less common, although not commanding higher prices, are examples with either a blank reverse or the words ''MADE IN USA.'' The buttons were distributed sealed in a small paper wrapper in cereal boxes from approximately 1945 to 1947. In excellent condition, with near perfect paint, the average retail value is $10 each. However, double the value for Denny, Gravel Gertie, Mac, Snuffy Smith, Tiny Tim, and Winnie's Twins. Triple the value for Felix The Cat and The Phantom. Superman is the most common button in the set, as it was included each time a new group was issued over the two-year period.

10
"KEWPIE" 2.5″ tall painted bisque figure depicted holding parasol and traveling case. Japanese c. 1930s. $250

11
KEWPIE 1x1x2.25″ tall china perfume vial by Goebel of Germany c. early 1930s. $75

12
KEWPIE 3x3x3.5″ tall single unit molded glass candy container with painted Kewpie figure. By George Borgfeldt c. 1920s or later. $150

13
KEWPIE 7″ tall painted plaster lamp base figure with added 3″ brass bulb socket. c. 1930s. $75

14
KEWPIE 3.5x5″ Limoges white china tray with soft color art c. 1920s. $50

15
"KEWPIES" 3.5x5.5″ full color Christmas postcard c. 1925. $15

16
"THE KEWPIES/THEIR BOOK" 8x11″ hard cover with 80 pages of verse and pictures by Rose O'Neill published by Frederick Stokes Co. © 1913. Example photo shows front cover, inside end papers, frontispiece. $250

17
"THE KEWPIES AND DOTTY DARLING" 8x11″ hard cover book of verse and pictures by Rose O'Neill published by George Doran Co. © 1912. Example photo shows front cover and inside end papers. $250

18
"KEWPIE" 3x5.5″ full color "Victory Ice Cream" postcard from series of seven for that product © 1920. $25

19
"KEWPIE-KIN PAPERDOLLS" 8.25x12.25″ Saalfield book © 1967. $40

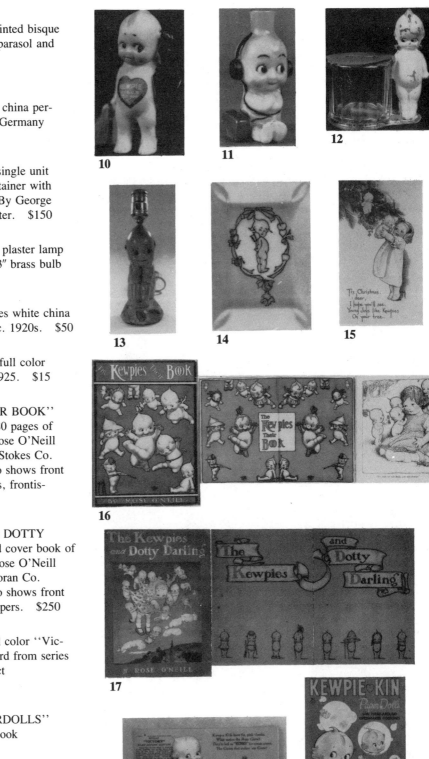

Krazy Kat

Creator: George Herriman

Began: (D) 6/20/10; (S) 4/23/16. Hearst Syndicate.

Principal Characters: Krazy Kat, Ignatz, Officer Pupp, Archy (cockroach).

Synopsis: Classic cat (Krazy) vs. mouse (Ignatz) comedy strip that originated under title *The Dingbat Family* before gaining its final title circa 1913. The traditional plot involved the affection for Krazy by Officer Pupp, both hounded by Ignatz, a no-nonsense mouse which usually expressed his displeasure by heaving a brick. The strip was equally known for language dialect variations interjected by Herriman. The strip was discontinued with Herriman's death in 1944.

1

2

3

4

5

1

"KRAZY KAT" 18″ tall stuffed felt doll with original tag on back for Averill Mfg. Co. c. 1920s. $500

2

"IGNATZ MOUSE" 7″ long by 10″ tall wood and tin mechanical toy with paper bellows that squeak. Made and marked by J. Chein & Co. © 1932. $1000

3

"KRAZY KAT EXPRESS" 4x5x12″ long wooden pull toy with tin title plate on front by maker J. Chein & Co. © 1932. $1500

4

"IGNATZ" 5.5″ tall bw painted wood figure with fabric over flexible wire arms, legs and tail. Name sticker is on chest. Figure is in 2x2x6″ wide box by Cameo Doll Co. distributed by George Borgfeldt c. 1930s.   BOXED $500, UNBOXED $300

5

KRAZY KAT ORIGINAL ART by George Herriman inked in black on 7.5x23″ white art sheet for daily strip scheduled for publication June 1, 1931. $750

6
"KRAZY KAT KIDDIES KLUB"
4x6.5" full color membership card
c. 1920s. $300

7
KRAZY KAT 1.25" tall enameled
metal pin with rhinestone eyes
c. 1930s. $35

8
"KRAZY KAT IN AN AWFUL
SPOOK" 16mm home film in 1x4x4"
box. By Keystone Co. c. 1930s. $35

9
"KRAZY KAT KANNIBALS" 8mm
bw home movie film in 1x4x4" box
© 1913 but c. late 1940s. $35

10
"KRAZY KAT" sweatshirt with 5"
tall printed image on chest.
c. 1930s. $75

11
KRAZY & IGNATZ "IN KOKO
LAND" 3.5x8" Saalfield book #1056
© 1934. $150

12
"KRAZY KAT" 9x11" book of
comic strip reprints published by Holt
& Co. © 1946. $75

13
KRAZY KAT "JAZZ-PANTOM-
IME" 9x12" folio with 1948 revised
version of original 1922 souvenir program for Krazy/Ignatz live pantomime
stage production in New York City.
Example photo shows cover, title
page, typical art page. $200

14
KRAZY KAT "CONNECT DOTS"
8x11" activity book by Lowe & Co.
© 1963. $20

15
KRAZY KAT 6x8.5" original art
inked in black on white sheet for
1960s coloring book by unidentified
artist. $35

16
KRAZY KAT 6x8.5" original art
inked in black on white sheet for
1960s coloring book by unidentified
artist. $35

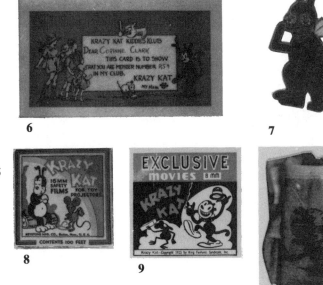

6

7

8

9

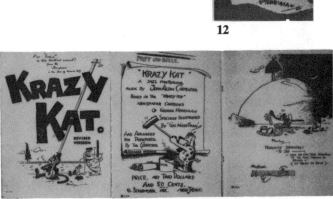

10

11

12

13

14

15

16

Li'l Abner

Creator: Al Capp

Began: (D) 8/20/34; (S) 2/24/35. United Features Syndicate.

Principal Characters: Abner Yokum, Daisy Mae, Mammy and Pappy Yokum, Marryin' Sam, Sadie Hawkins, Fearless Fosdick, Hairless Joe, Lonesome Polecat, Salomey (pig), Cedric Cesspool, Moonbeam McSwine, Shmoos, Kigmys, many more.

Synopsis: Long-running comedy, pun and parody strip set in the backwoods community of Dogpatch; well known for its satire characterizations of actual individuals. The strip was adapted to a 1940 movie, a late 1950s stage musical, and a 1959 movie version. The strip continued under Capp's guidance with several contributing artists until 1977.

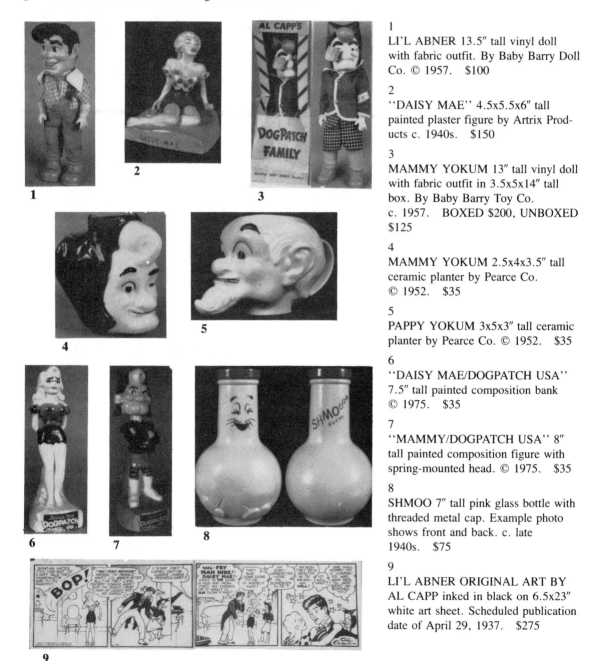

1
LI'L ABNER 13.5″ tall vinyl doll with fabric outfit. By Baby Barry Doll Co. © 1957. $100

2
"DAISY MAE" 4.5x5.5x6″ tall painted plaster figure by Artrix Products c. 1940s. $150

3
MAMMY YOKUM 13″ tall vinyl doll with fabric outfit in 3.5x5x14″ tall box. By Baby Barry Toy Co. c. 1957. BOXED $200, UNBOXED $125

4
MAMMY YOKUM 2.5x4x3.5″ tall ceramic planter by Pearce Co. © 1952. $35

5
PAPPY YOKUM 3x5x3″ tall ceramic planter by Pearce Co. © 1952. $35

6
"DAISY MAE/DOGPATCH USA" 7.5″ tall painted composition bank © 1975. $35

7
"MAMMY/DOGPATCH USA" 8″ tall painted composition figure with spring-mounted head. © 1975. $35

8
SHMOO 7″ tall pink glass bottle with threaded metal cap. Example photo shows front and back. c. late 1940s. $75

9
LI'L ABNER ORIGINAL ART BY AL CAPP inked in black on 6.5x23″ white art sheet. Scheduled publication date of April 29, 1937. $275

10

"DOGPATCH BAND" 6x9x8.5″ tall tin wind-up toy by Unique Art Mfg. Co. c. 1946-1948.   BOXED $800, UNBOXED $600

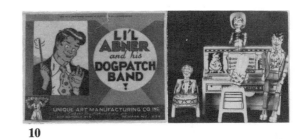

10

11

"LI'L ABNER AND LONESOME POLECAT CANOE" 3x3.5x12″ long plastic wind-up toy c. late 1940s. BOXED $200, UNBOXED $150

11

12

"QUICK" 4x6″ pocket magazine for Jan. 23, 1950. $10

13

"LI'L ABNER" 8x11″ Saalfield coloring book #209 © 1941. $40

14

"LI'L ABNER AND DAISY MAE" 11x12.5″ Saalfield paperdoll book #215. © 1941. $125

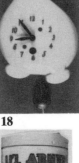

12

13

14

15

"THE LI'L ABNER GAME" by Parker Bros. © 1969 in 1.5x9x17″ wide box. $40

16

SHMOO FAMILY set of six plastic nesting figures with tallest being 5.5″. c. late 1940s.   SET $125

15

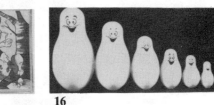

16

17

SHMOO 6.5″ tall ceramic deodorizer figure with wick for deodorizing fluid. c. late 1940s. $125

18

SHMOO 2x4x6″ tall white plastic key-wind wall clock by Lux Co. c. late 1940s. $200

19

SHMOO 3x4.5x7″ tall white plastic bank © 1948. $65

20

SHMOO 1.5x1.5x2.25″ tall set of white china salt and pepper shakers with softly tinted heads. c. late 1940s.   SET $150

17

18

19

21

"LI'L ABNER'S CAN O'COINS" 4.5″ tall lithographed tin canister bank © 1953 with other character depictions on reverse. $100

22

"KIGMY" 4.5″ tall plastic spring operated toy that sits then jumps by spring action. c. late 1940s. $75

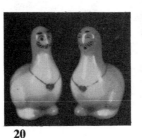

20

21

22

Little Annie Rooney

Creator: Ed Verdier (Verd), Ben Batsford

Began: (D) 1/10/29. (S) circa 1934. King Features Syndicate.

Later Artists and/or Writers: Brandon Walsh (writer), various artists starting with Darrell McClure.

Principal Characters: Annie Rooney, her dog Zero, Mrs. Meany.

Synopsis: Daily and Sunday strip developed as competitor to Little Orphan Annie, although without the far-reaching international story plots. Rooney's perils almost always began and ended with an optimistic assessment. Her favorite exclamation, in a similar vein to Orphan Annie's "Leapin' Lizards" was "Gloryosky." The strip continued until 1966.

1

2

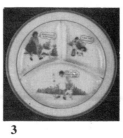

3

1
"LITTLE ANNIE ROONEY" 17″ tall jointed composition doll with fabric outfit tagged by maker Jack Collins © 1925. $250

2
"ANNIE ROONEY" 5″ tall painted composition wood figure © 1944. $50

3
LITTLE ANNIE ROONEY/ZERO 8″ diameter child's china plate with molded divider sections and colored art. Made in Japan © 1935. $50

4

4
LITTLE ANNIE ROONEY/ZERO 3″ tall double-handled white china mug with full color art. Made in Japan © 1935. $50

5
"LITTLE ANNIE ROONEY AND THE ORPHAN HOUSE" Whitman Big Little Book #1117 © 1936. $25

6
"LITTLE ANNIE ROONEY ON THE HIGHWAY TO ADVENTURE" Whitman Big Little Book #1406 © 1938. $25

5

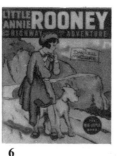

6

7
"LITTLE ANNIE ROONEY PAINT BOOK" 11x14″ with 96 pages pub-lished by Whitman © 1935. $35

8
"LITTLE ANNIE ROONEY WISH-ING BOOK" 10x13″ with 20 pages published by McLoughlin Bros. © 1932. $35

7

8

9

9
"ANNIE ROONEY" 8.5x11.5″ Fea-ture Book #11 by David McKay Co. © 1937. $120

The Little King

Creator: Otto Soglow

Began: (S) 9/9/34. King Features Syndicate.

Principal Characters: Little King and Family.

Synopsis: Diminutive, unnamed and mute king whose popularity lasted over 40 years despite an unnamed kingdom, unnamed wife and daughter and unnamed other strip visitors, all essentially mute. The strip continued until Soglow's death in 1975.

1
"LITTLE KING" 2.5″ tall painted composition wood figure
© 1944. $150

2
"THE LITTLE KING" 4″ tall painted wood spool toy in 2.5x2.5x4″ tall bwr box. By Jaymar © 1939. BOXED $125, UNBOXED $70

3
"THE LITTLE KING" 8x11″ book published by John Martin House
© 1945. $35

4
"THE LITTLE KING" 8.5x11″ book of New Yorker Magazine cartoon reprints © 1933 prior to newspaper strip syndication. $50

5
THE LITTLE KING 3.25x5.25″ department store Christmas folder picturing gift possibilities c. 1940s. $20

6
THE LITTLE KING 4″ diameter full color metal purse compact with art on lid and bottom. c. 1940s. $250

7
LITTLE KING & COMPANION 1.5x3x3″ tall full color plastic ramp walker toy by Marx Toys
c. 1950s. $50

8
THE LITTLE KING ORIGINAL ART BY O. SOGLOW inked in black on 13.5x20.5″ white art sheet with scheduled newspaper publication date of Sunday, September 18, 1938. $450

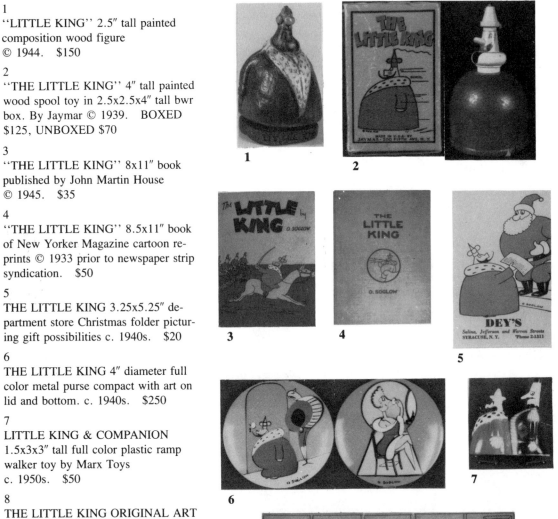

Little Lulu

Creator: Marge (Marjorie Henderson Buell)

Began: 6/50, Chicago Tribune-New York News Syndicate.

Later Artists and/or Writers: Woody Kimbrell, Del Connell, Roger Armstrong.

Principal Characters: Lulu Moppet, Tubby Tompkins, Alvin, Wilbur Van Snobbe.

Synopsis: Usually silent but ever-ingenuous little girl dating from mid-1930s appearances in *The Saturday Evening Post*. Prior to the newspaper strip, Lulu was very popular in comic books and also well known from 1944 through 1960 from ads for Kleenex facial tissues. Most of Lulu publications after the mid-1940s were done by other artists under the Buell name. Newspaper publication ceased in the late 1960s.

1

2

3

1
"LITTLE LULU" 15″ tall cloth doll with molded linen face, black yarn hair, plastic purse. © 1944. $175

2
LULU 15″ tall cloth doll in cowgirl outfit c. 1944. $250

3
LULU 3.75″ tall china figurine. Occupied Japan c. late 1940s. $100

4

5

6

4
LITTLE LULU 15″ tall inflatible vinyl doll © 1973. $30

5
TUBBY & LULU 2.75″ tall bisque figures © 1975.   EACH $40

6
LITTLE LULU 8″ tall painted vinyl bank c. 1970s. $25

7
LITTLE LULU Whitman Better Little Book #1429 © 1947. $35

7

8

9

8
"FUN WITH LITTLE LULU" 7x8.25″ 1944 reprint book of original © 1936 cartoons from Saturday Evening Post. $40

9
"ON PARADE" 7x8.5″ cartoon reprint book © 1941. $40

10
"THE ORGAN GRINDER MAN" 7.5x9″ book © 1946. $35

10

11

12

11
"LITTLE LULU AT THE SEASHORE" 7.5x9″ book © 1946. $35

12
"LITTLE LULU PLAYS PIRATE" 7.5x9″ book © 1946. $35

13
"LITTLE LULU AND TUBBY TOM" 8.25x11.25″ Whitman coloring book © 1946. $40

14
"LITTLE LULU" 8.5x11″ Whitman coloring book © 1946. $30

15
"LITTLE LULU" 8.5x1″ Whitman coloring book © 1955. $30

16
LITTLE LULU "McCALL" magazine paper pattern for doll clothing © 1948 in 6x9″ envelope. $40

17
LITTLE LULU/KLEENEX TISSUES 11x14″ rwb cardboard display sign © 1952. $50

18
"LITTLE LULU/KLEENEX TISSUES" 10″ tall rwb diecut cardboard store display sign c. 1952. $35

19
LITTLE LULU & FRIENDS "CARTOON-A-KIT" stencil set in 1.25x10x14″ wide box © 1948. $75

20
"TUBBY TOM/FLIPPER" 4.75″ tall glass tumbler from set of six c. 1940s. $75

21
"ALVIN/GUNK" 4.75″ tall glass tumbler from set of six c. 1940s. $75

22
"LITTLE LULU" 6″ tall cologne bottle in 2x3.5x7.5″ tall box © 1958. $60

23
"LITTLE LULU ADVENTURE GAME" by Milton Bradley © 1945 in 1.5x15.5x21″ wide box. $50

13   14   15

16   17   18

19

20   21

22

23

Little Nemo in Slumberland

Creator: Winsor McCay

Began: (S) 10/15/05. New York Herald.

Principal Characters: Nemo, Flip, Impy, King Morpheous, Doctor Pill.

Synopsis: Universally acclaimed dream fantasy adventure strip rendered in beautiful art nouveau draftsmanship and choice use of color. The strip alternated between news syndicates until 1927 with a brief reprinting revival in the late 1940s.

1
LITTLE NEMO 11.5x16.5″ comic strip reprint book by Cupples & Leon Co. © 1909. Example photo is missing cover and shows title page plus sample page.   COMPLETE $400

2
''LITTLE NEMO'' 10.5x14″ sheet music © 1908 with full color cover art. $75

3
''LITTLE NEMO/A FAIRY TALE'' 10.25x13.5″ sheet music with rwb cover art by Casseau rather than McKay © 1926. $60

4
LITTLE NEMO ''WONDERFUL DREAMS WITH MOTHER GOOSE'' 16.5x21.5″ full color comic strip from May 19, 1912 New York American. Example photo shows complete strip and first panel detail. $25

5
''LITTLE NEMO'' 3.5x6.5″ postcard fold-out mailer for New York stage play based on comic strips c. 1909. Example photo shows both opened sides plus Nemo picture detail. $100

6
"LITTLE NEMO CHILD'S SET" of
silverplate tableware in illustrated
1.5x3x8" tall box c. 1910. $60

7
LITTLE NEMO "VALENTINE
GREETINGS" 3.5x5" full color card
by Raphael Tuck from © 1907 set by
New York Herald. $35

8
FROM SAME SET AS #7. $35

9
FROM SAME SET AS #7. $35

10
FROM SAME SET AS #7. $35

11
FROM SAME SET AS #7. $35

12
FROM SAME SET AS #7. $35

13
FROM SAME SET AS #7. $35

14
FROM SAME SET AS #7. $35

15
"LITTLE NEMO IN SLUMBER-
LAND" 5.5x6.5" Rand McNally book
adapted from original cartoons
© 1941. Example photo shows front
cover and typical full color story
page. $90

16
"STAR COMICS" issue #4 for June
1937 with full color Little Nemo art
and stories by McCay. $185

17
"LITTLE NEMO IN SLUMBER-
LAND" 7x11" comic strip reprint
book © 1945 of bw examples of original 1905-1911 New York Herald
strips. $35

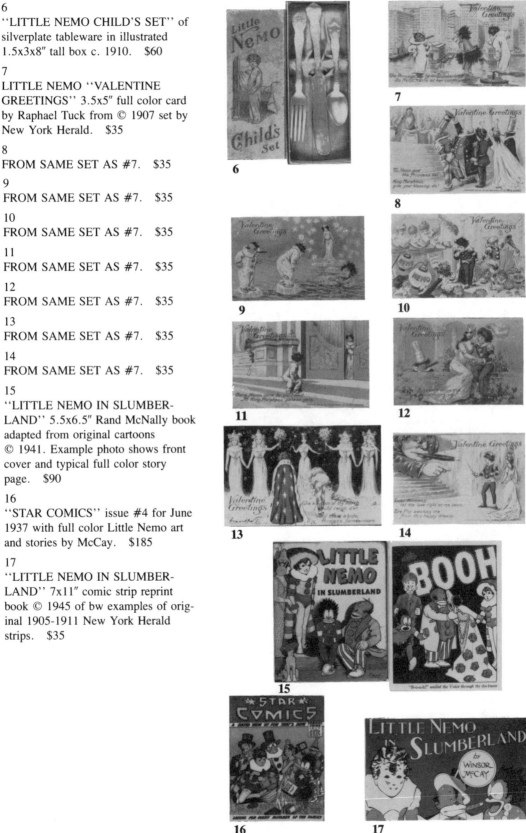

Little Orphan Annie

Creator: Harold Gray

Began: (D) 8/5/24. Chicago Tribune-New York News Syndicate.

Later Artists and/or Writers: Robert Leffingwell, Henri Arnold, Henry Raduta, Tex Blaisdell, Elliott Caplin, David Lettick.

Principal Characters: Orphan Annie, Sandy, Daddy Warbucks, Punjab, Asp.

Synopsis: One of the most famous comic strips ever, with Annie's popularity heightened by many years of association with Ovaltine, the sponsor of her radio version. Her long newspaper strip career culminated in the mid-1970s with the reprinting of original strips from nearly 40 years earlier. A musical stage version followed in 1977 and a movie version in the early 1980s.

1

2

3

4

5

6

7

8

9

10

11

12

1
HAROLD GRAY 7x9″ Christmas card. 1928. $100

2
HAROLD GRAY 3x5″ Christmas card. 1948. $100

3
HAROLD GRAY 5x7″ Christmas card. 1967. $100

4
OILCLOTH DOLL with 17″ Annie in fabric dress. Sandy is 8.5″ tall. 1930s.   ANNIE $300, SANDY $150

5
FABRIC DOLLS 8″ tall and 6″ tall dolls c. 1930s.   EACH $150

6
WARBUCKS 3.5″ tall German bisque nodder. 1930s. $90

7
"LITTLE ORPHAN ANNIE" 5″ tall tin wind-up by Marx c. 1931. $600

8
"SANDY" 3″ tall tin wind-up with bookbag. Marx 1931. $400

9
"LITTLE ORPHAN ANNIE" 10x13″ sheet music from first year of newspaper syndication © 1925. $75

10
SONG FOLIO 9x12″ with Anne Gillis, Paramount movie © 1938. $90

11
"LITTLE ORPHAN ANNIE" 8.5x11″ comic strip reprint book by Cupples & Leon Co. © 1926. $50

12
"LITTLE ORPHAN ANNIE" 8.5x11″ comic strip reprint book by Cupples & Leon Co. © 1929. $50

13
ANNIE/JUMBO, THE CIRCUS ELE-
PHANT 8.5x10″ pop-up picture book
© 1935. $175

14
ANNIE "JUNIOR COMMANDOS"
11x14″ Saalfield paperdoll book
© 1943.   UNCUT $150

15
ANNIE paperdolls by Gabriel in
1x8x10″ tall box c. 1930s.   UNCUT
$150

16
ANNIE "BIG LITTLE KIT" 4x6″
box of 384 bw coloring pictures
© 1937. $125

17
"LITTLE ORPHAN ANNIE WITH
THE CIRCUS" Whitman Big Little
Book © 1934. $35

18
"LITTLE ORPHAN ANNIE AND
THE BIG TOWN GUNMAN" 5.5x8″
Whitman book © 1937. $75

19
ANNIE 11x14″ McLoughlin Bros.
coloring book © 1933. $50

20
ANNIE 10x15″ McLoughlin Bros.
coloring book c. mid-1930s. $50

21
ANNIE 8.5x10″ Popped Wheat premium comic book c. 1947. $10

22
"LITTLE ORPHAN ANNIE'S
SONG" 10x12″ bw sheet music pre-
mium by Ovaltine © 1931. $25

23
ROA 6x9″ Ovaltine first manual premium for 1934. $50

24
ROA 6x9″ Ovaltine premium manual
for 1935. $60

25
ROA 6x9″ Ovaltine premium manual
for 1936. $50

26
ROA 6x9″ Ovaltine premium manual
for 1937. $50

27
ROA 6x9″ Ovaltine premium manual
for 1938. $60

13

14

15

16

17

18

19

20

21

22

23

24

25

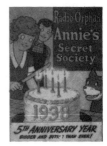

26

27

28

29

30

31

32

33   **34**

35

36   **37**

38   **39**   **40**

28
ROA 6x9″ Ovaltine premium manual for 1939. $70

29
ROA 6x9″ Ovaltine premium manual for 1940. $70

30
ANNIE "SECRET GUARD" 8.5x11″ manual and Slidomatic decoder set by Quaker Puffed Wheat & Rice from 1942.   MANUAL $100, DECODER $50

31
ROA "WELCOME TO SIMMONS CORNERS" 19x24″ Ovaltine premium map c. 1936. Photo shows total map and title detail from it. $75

32
ROA "GOOFY CIRCUS" 10x14″ punch-out book from Ovaltine c. 1936.   UNPUNCHED $250

33
ROA 3″ tall ceramic first Ovaltine mug premium c. 1932. $50

34
ROA 3″ tall beetleware plastic mug with decal, Ovaltine premium c. 1935. $50

35
ROA OVALTINE 5″ tall white beetleware plastic shake-up mug c. 1931. $60

36
ROA OVALTINE 5″ tall white beetleware plastic shake-up mug c. 1935. $75

37
ROA OVALTINE 5″ tall blue beetleware plastic shake-up mug c. 1938. $90

38
ROA OVALTINE 5″ tall brown beetleware plastic shake-up mug c. 1939. $90

39
ROA OVALTINE 5″ tall green beetleware plastic shake-up mug c. 1940. $90

40
OVALTINE "GOLDEN ANNIE-VERSARY" 3.5″ tall white ceramic 50th year commemorative mug © 1981. $25

41
ROA & JOE CORNTASSEL set of
8x10″ bw Ovaltine premium photos
c. 1932. SET $40

42
ROA "SHADOWETTS" set of six
paper mechanical portraits, each 3x5″,
in mailing envelope. Ovaltine premium c. 1938. SET $90

43
ANNIE "RADIO-PHONE" 3.5x5x̄4″
tall red bakelite replica telephone
holding battery operated radio. In
original box c. late 1930s. $250

44
ANNIE .5x3″ diameter tin dime register bank © 1936. $300

45
ANNIE "TEA SET" of dark green
Depression glass c. 1930s in 3x13x13″
box. $150

46
ANNIE "PASTRY SET" of toy
cooking utensils in 2.5x6x8″ wide box
c. 1930s. $85

47
ANNIE "JACK SET" of rubber ball
and metal toy jacks on 5x7″ card
c. 1930s. $50

48
ANNIE "BUBBLE SET" of equipment for blowing soap bubbles in
1.5x5x9″ wide box c. 1930s. $75

49
ANNIE GAME with playing board in
2x9x17″ wide box c. 1930s. $90

50
ANNIE "TRAVEL" GAME with
playing board on bottom of 2x8x14″
wide box. c. 1930s. $75

51
ANNIE "TO THE RESCUE" GAME
with playing board printed on bottom
of 2x8x14″ wide box. c. 1930s. $75

52
ANNIE "SHOOTING" Milton Bradley target game in 2x9x12″ wide box
c. 1930s. $100

53
ANNIE "RUMMY CARDS" Whit-
man © 1935 game in 1x3.5x5″ wide
box. $50

41

42

43

44

45

46

47

48

49

50

51

52

53

The Lone Ranger

Creator: Fran Striker (writer), Ed Kressy (artist)

Began: (S) 9/10/38, King Features Syndicate.

Later Artists and/or Writers: Jon Blummer, Charles Flanders, Paul Newman, Russ Heath, Cary Bates.

Principal Characters: Lone Ranger, horse Silver, companion Tonto, horse Scout.

Synopsis: Newspaper strip based on the impetus from early 1930s radio broadcasts, movie serials, novels, dime books about the masked man and his Indian sidekick.   The strip ended in 1971 but was revived for about three years beginning in 1981 under new artists.

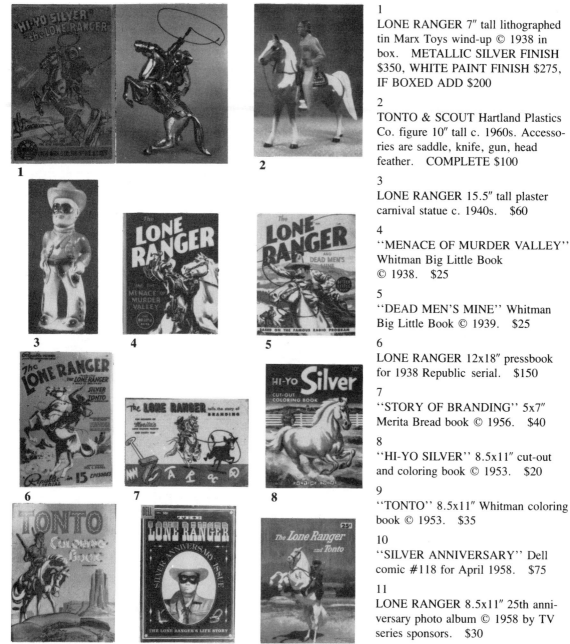

1
LONE RANGER 7″ tall lithographed tin Marx Toys wind-up © 1938 in box.   METALLIC SILVER FINISH $350, WHITE PAINT FINISH $275, IF BOXED ADD $200

2
TONTO & SCOUT Hartland Plastics Co. figure 10″ tall c. 1960s. Accessories are saddle, knife, gun, head feather.   COMPLETE $100

3
LONE RANGER 15.5″ tall plaster carnival statue c. 1940s. $60

4
''MENACE OF MURDER VALLEY'' Whitman Big Little Book © 1938. $25

5
''DEAD MEN'S MINE'' Whitman Big Little Book © 1939. $25

6
LONE RANGER 12x18″ pressbook for 1938 Republic serial. $150

7
''STORY OF BRANDING'' 5x7″ Merita Bread book © 1956. $40

8
''HI-YO SILVER'' 8.5x11″ cut-out and coloring book © 1953. $20

9
''TONTO'' 8.5x11″ Whitman coloring book © 1953. $35

10
''SILVER ANNIVERSARY'' Dell comic #118 for April 1958. $75

11
LONE RANGER 8.5x11″ 25th anniversary photo album © 1958 by TV series sponsors. $30

12
LONE RANGER FREE PONY CON-
TEST 11x14″ cardboard display sign
c. 1930s. $150

13
LONE RANGER/BOND BREAD
8x12″ advertising handbill
© 1938. $90

14
LONE RANGER "CHIEF SCOUT"
set of five 3.75x7.5″ consecutive
"Degree" cards to be completed for
earning Chief Scout Safety Badge
c. 1934-1938. EACH $60

15
LONE RANGER/SILVERCUP
BREAD "HUNT MAP" 13x17″ premium in 8x13″ envelope c. late
1930s. MAP $150, ENVELOPE $50

16
LONE RANGER ORIGINAL COMIC
STRIP ART by Charles Flanders
inked in black on 6.25x19.5″ white art
sheet for publication Dec. 19,
1959. $125

17
LONE RANGER Dell Comics premium folder sheet that opens to
8.25x33″ with five full color pictures.
© 1951. Example photo shows two
pictures from folder. $100

18
LONE RANGER & TONTO 8x10″
full color picture with facsimile signa-
tures c. early 1950s. $10

19
LONE RANGER & TONTO life-sized
25x74″ tall full color portrait posters
offered as Wheaties premiums
c. 1957. EACH $150

12

13

14

15

16

17

18

19

20

21

22

23

24

25

26

27

28

29

30

31

20
LONE RANGER 10″ long leather gun holster and belt set with black horse-hair accent on holster.   In 1.5x5x10″ tall box c. 1939. $100

21
LONE RANGER 6x9x15″ wide dark brown plastic table model radio by Pilot Co. c. 1939. $800

22
LONE RANGER pocketwatch with miniature metal gun and leather holster strap fob in .5x3.5x4″ tall box © 1940 by New Haven Clock Co.   BOX $150, WATCH $300

23
"LONE RANGER FIRST AID KIT" in 2x5x7″ wide tin box. © 1938. $25

24
LONE RANGER 8″ long "Flashlight Pistol" by Marx Toys in 2x6x11″ box c. early 1950s.   BOXED $200, LOOSE $125

25
LONE RANGER 7x8x4″ deep flat steel lunch box by ADCO Liberty © 1954.   RED SIDES $250, BLUE SIDES $400

26
LONE RANGER 1x4x5″ Milton Bradley lithographed tin paint box with contents c. 1950s. $25

27
"LONE RANGER STORY PUZ-ZLE" 1x7x19″ wide box holding four jigsaw puzzles forming complete story. 1950s. $90

28
"LONE RANGER RODEO" playset by Marx Toys c. 1950 in 3x13x15″ wide box.   COMPLETE $200

29
LONE RANGER 11x17″ full color lithographed tin target with gun and darts by Marx Toys © 1939. $75

30
LONE RANGER 4.25″ wide plastic harmonica on 4x4.5″ diecut card c. 1950s. $40

31
TONTO 4.5″ diameter by 6″ tall metal drum with rubber drum heads plus wood drumsticks. c. 1950s. $75

Mandrake the Magician

Creator: Lee Falk (writer) and Phil Davis (artist)

Began: (D) 6/11/34; (S) 2/3/35. King Features Syndicate.

Later Artists and/or Writers: Fred Fredericks.

Principal Characters: Mandrake, Lothar.

Synopsis: Enduring strip featuring debonair, charming magician able to quell evil-doers through magical and illusion powers plus hypnotism. He is ably assisted in his adventures by black companion Lothar, who is capable of more direct strong-armed tactics.

1
MANDRAKE 8x10″ bw Christmas card with facsimile greetings from Lee Falk and Phil Davis c. 1940s. $30

2
"MANDRAKE THE MAGICIAN/ THE MIGHTY SOLVER OF MYS-TERIES" Whitman Better Little Book #1454 © 1941. $30

3
"MANDRAKE THE MAGICIAN AND THE FLAME PEARLS" Whitman Better Little Book #1418 © 1946. $25

4
MANDRAKE comic Feature Book #18 c. 1938. $135

5
MANDRAKE comic Feature Book #19 © 1938. $135

6
MANDRAKE 8.5x11″ coloring book by Ottenheimer Co. © 1965. $15

7
MANDRAKE "MAGIC KIT" by Transogram © 1951 in 2.5x11.5x17.5″ box. $125

8
MANDRAKE ORIGINAL COMIC STRIP ART inked in black on 17.5x24.5″ white art sheet for publication date of Sunday, June 17, 1951. $60

9
MANDRAKE game by Transogram © 1966 in 1.5x7x15″ wide box. $40

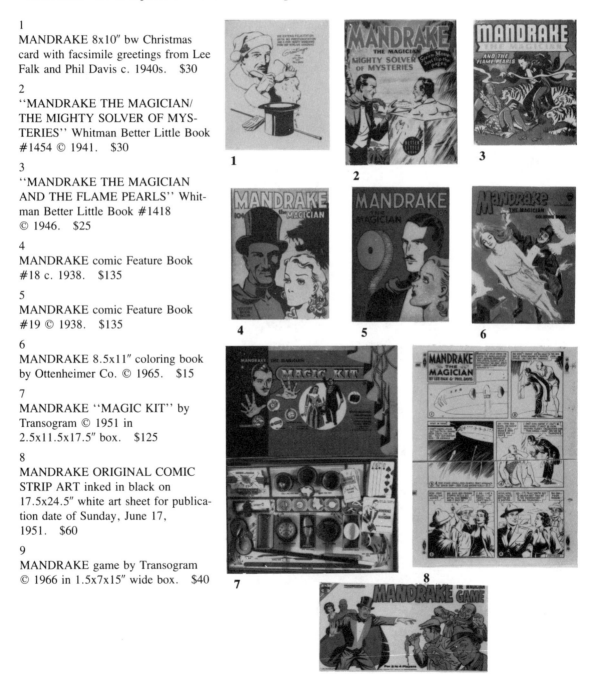

Mickey Mouse

Creator: Walt Disney and Ub Iwerks, Win Smith (artists)

Began: (D) 1/13/30; (S) 1/10/32. King Features Syndicate.

Later Artists and/or Writers: Floyd Gottfredson, Manuel Gonzalez, many others.

Principal Characters: Mickey Mouse, Minnie Mouse.

Synopsis: The most internationally known comic character, Mickey's daily newspaper strip was done chiefly by Floyd Gottfredson from the early 1930s into the mid-1970s. The pre-1950 era is generally considered the outstanding Mickey comic strip years, as he forged through a spectrum of perilous adventures. The later years, reputedly at the behest of King Features Syndicate, slowed Mickey's ventures in favor of a more sedate joke narrative format.

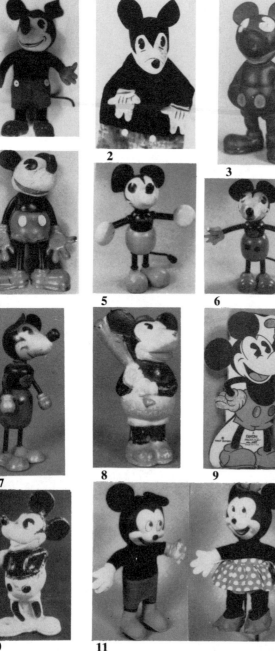

1
MICKEY 12″ tall cloth doll with composition feet by Knickerbocker 1930s. $400

2
MICKEY 10″ tall cloth hand puppet by Steiff 1930s. $600

3
MICKEY 3.5″ tall rubber figure by Seiberling 1930s. $100

4
MICKEY 6″ tall rubber figure by Seiberling 1930s. $175

5
MICKEY 7″ tall jointed wood figure 1930s. $600

6
MICKEY 7″ tall wood figure with flexible wire arms by Fun-E-Flex 1930s. $500

7
MICKEY 4″ tall wood figure with wire flexible arms by Fun-E-Flex 1930s.   MICKEY $150, MINNIE (NOT SHOWN) $125

8
''MICKEY BATTER'' 3.25″ tall painted bisque figure from baseball set of four also including pitcher, catcher, fielder. 1930s.   EACH $150

9
MICKEY 5x8.5″ tall cardboard pencil box by Dixon 1930s. $400

10
MICKEY 5″ tall composition pencil holder by Dixon 1930s. $300

11
MICKEY, MINNIE 13″ tall cloth doll set by Gund c. late 1940s.   MICKEY $125, MINNIE $100

12
MICKEY 6.5″ tall celluloid toy with removable head © 1930. $700

13
MICKEY ON HORSE 3x6″ tall by 7″ long celluloid wind-up
c. 1930s. $800

14
MICKEY RACER 2x2x4″ long tin wind-up 1930s. $300

15
MICKEY DRUMMER 11″ tall tin battery toy by Linemar
c. 1950s. $350

16
DISNEYLAND FERRIS WHEEL 5x11x17″ tall tin wind-up by Chein 1950s. $300

17
MICKEY first book 9x12″ by Bibo & Lang book © 1930. $700

18
MICKEY 10x10″ Series No. 1 book by David McKay © 1931. $300

19
MICKEY 9.5x10″ Book No. 2 by David McKay © 1932. $250

20
MICKEY 9.5x10″ Book No. 3 by David McKay © 1933. $200

21
MICKEY Whitman Big Little Book © 1933. $150

22
MICKEY Whitman Big Little Book © 1933. $125

23
MICKEY 5.5x8″ Book 1 by McKay © 1931. $100

24
MICKEY MAGAZINE 10x13.5″ Vol. 1 #1 © 1935. $400

25
MICKEY MOVIE STORIES 6x8.5″ book by McKay © 1931. $250

26
MICKEY PAINT BOOK 9x11″ by Saalfield © 1931. $175

27
GUM CARD ALBUM 6x10″ Vol. 2 from set of two. 1930s.   VOL. I (NOT SHOWN) $100, VOL. II $150

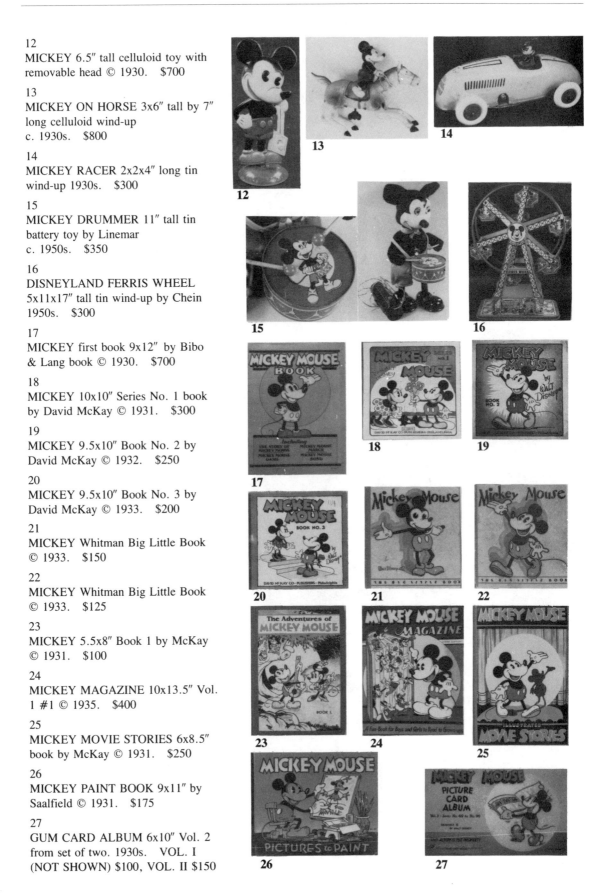

28

29

30

31

32

33

34

35

36

37

38

39

40

41

42

28
MICKEY 10x15″ coloring book by Saalfield © 1931. $90

29
MICKEY 10x19″ cut-out doll book by Saalfield © 1933. $300

30
MICKEY 3.5x5.5″ bw first newspaper premium card. 1931. $300

31
MICKEY 7x9″ bw probable first studio fan card c. early 1930s. $250

32
MICKEY 2.25x2.75″ movie theatre club membership card with creed on back. Early 1930s. $100

33
MICKEY 6x8″ school composition book © 1930. $150

34
MICKEY 10x13″ bwr sheet music © 1932. $150

35
MICKEY BIRTHDAY PARTY 10x13″ blw/orange sheet music © 1936. $60

36
MICKEY 4x6″ Christmas card mid-1930s. $50

37
MICKEY, MINNIE 10x12″ paper masks often toy store premiums © 1933.   EACH $65

38
MICKEY 11x14″ set of four tray puzzles in box by Marks © 1934. BOXED SET $400, EACH $75

39
MICKEY/MINNIE 8″ diameter china divided feeding dish 1930s. $150

40
MICKEY 6x9″ cardboard pencil box by Dixon c. 1935. $100

41
"MICKEY MOUSE LUNCH KIT" 5″ tall by 8″ long tin box by Geuder, Paeschke & Frey c. 1935. $1200

42
DISNEY SCHOOL BUS 6.5″ tall by 9″ long steel dome lunch box with bottle by Aladdin © 1961.   BOX $45, BOTTLE $20

43
FIRST POCKETWATCH by Ingersoll.
Mickey image on reverse. 1933. $400

44
MICKEY first wristwatch by Ingersoll. Leather or metal straps.
1933. $300

45
MICKEY wristwatch by Ingersoll
1947. $125

46
MICKEY wristwatch by Ingersoll
1949. $90

47
MICKEY 2.25″ deep by 4.5″ square
earliest wind-up alarm by Ingersoll,
also produced in electric version.
WIND-UP $500, ELECTRIC $800

48
MICKEY 2x4.5″ diameter wind-up
alarm clock by Bayard c. 1965.
BOXED $200, LOOSE $125

49
EMERSON RADIO 7x7x5″ deep
composition wood c. 1934. $1500

50
MICKEY 6x12x15″ tall metal movie
projector by Keystone with box
1930s.   BOXED $450, LOOSE $300

51
ATLANTIC CITY'' 6″ tall tin pail by
Ohio Art 1930s. $300

52
MICKEY PARTY GAME in 8x10″
envelope by Marks 1930s.   UNCUT
$150, CUT $75

53
MICKEY card game in 2.5x4″ box by
Whitman © 1934. $75

54
MICKEY FIRE DEPT. 2.5x4x6.5″
long by Sun Rubber 1940s. $75

55
MICKEY AIR MAIL 3.5x5x6.5″ long
by Sun Rubber. Photo example is
missing propeller. 1940s. $75

56
MICKEY 5x7x8″ long wood pull toy
by Fisher-Price 1949. $150

57
MOUSEKETEER EARS of plastic on
5x12 card. 1950s. $30

43

44

45   **46**

47   **48**

49   **50**

51   **52**   **53**

54   **55**

56

57

Moon Mullins

Creator: Frank Willard

Began: (D) 6/19/23; (S) 9/9/23. Chicago Tribune—New York News Syndicate.

Later Artists and/or Writers: Fred Johnson, Tom Johnson.

Principal Characters: Moon Mullins, Kayo, Emmy Schmaltz, Lord Plushbottom, Uncle Willie, Mamie.

Synopsis: Humorous character study of individuals living in boarding house run by Emmy. Brash Moon (short for Moonshine) and his cynical little brother Kayo are only rarely seen with their derby hats removed. Lord Plushbottom, eventually to wed Emmy, is a pretender aristocrat. Husband and wife Willie and Mamie rarely find any accord or harmony. The strip has been continued by Fred Johnson since Willard's death in 1958.

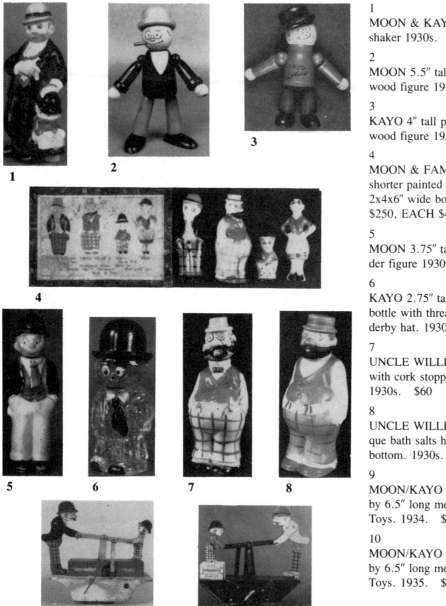

1
MOON & KAYO 3.5″ tall china salt shaker 1930s.   EACH $50, SET $125

2
MOON 5.5″ tall painted and jointed wood figure 1930s. $125

3
KAYO 4″ tall painted and jointed wood figure 1930s. $125

4
MOON & FAMILY 3.5″ tall or shorter painted bisque figure set in 2x4x6″ wide box 1930s.   BOXED $250, EACH $40

5
MOON 3.75″ tall painted bisque nodder figure 1930s. $75

6
KAYO 2.75″ tall clear glass perfume bottle with threaded black plastic derby hat. 1930s. $35

7
UNCLE WILLIE 6.5″ tall china bottle with cork stopper in neck. 1930s. $60

8
UNCLE WILLIE 7.5″ tall painted bisque bath salts holder figure corked in bottom. 1930s. $75

9
MOON/KAYO HANDCAR 2.5x6″ tall by 6.5″ long metal wind-up by Marx Toys. 1934. $500

10
MOON/KAYO HANDCAR 2.5x6″ tall by 6.5″ long metal wind-up by Marx Toys. 1935. $450

11
MOON "POLICE PATROL" TOOT-
SIETOY 2.5″ long painted metal car
with rocking action axle. 1930s. $275

12
KAYO "ICE COMPANY" TOOT-
SIETOY 2″ long painted metal truck
with rocking action axle.
1930s. $225

13
"MAMIE" TOOTSIETOY 2.5″ long
painted metal with rocking action
axle. 1930s. $250

14
MOON & KAYO 3.5″ tall painted
plaster salt and pepper set
1940s. $35

15
MOON/PLUSHBOTTOM TWINS
Whitman Big Little Book #1134
© 1935. $30

16
MOON/KAYO Whitman Big Little
Book #746 © 1933. $25

17
KAYO Whitman Big Little Book
#1180 © 1937. $25

18
MOON MULLINS 10x10″ Cupples &
Leon book © 1932. $60

19
MOON MULLINS 10x13″ Mc-
Loughlin paint book. Photo shows
cover and title page. © 1932. $35

20
KAYO CHOCOLATE 14x21.5″ cardboard store sign c. 1940s. $175

21
KAYO CHOCOLATE 14x27.5″ tin
sign c. 1930s. $200

22
KAYO CHOCOLATE 6x13.5″ embossed tin thermometer sign
c. 1930s. $125

23
MOON "AUTOMOBILE RACE"
1x7.5x13.5″ wide Milton Bradley
game. 1930s. $75

24
EMMY & LORD PLUSHBOTTOM
8x9″ cardboard masks from Wheaties
boxes c. 1950.   EACH $8

11

12

13

14

15   **16**   **17**

18

19

20   **21**   **22**

23

24

Mutt and Jeff

Creator: Bud (Henry Conway) Fisher

Began: 11/15/07. San Francisco Chronicle, later by Bell Syndicate, United Features Syndicate.

Later Artists and/or Writers: Billy Liverpool, Al Smith, Ken Kling, Ed Mack, George Breisacher.

Principal Characters: Mutt, Jeff, Mutt's son Cicero.

Synopsis: One of the few strips to equally feature two characters, the elongated Mutt and the shrimp-sized Jeff. The strip's original title was *A. Mutt* (A. for Augustus). Jeff was added in 1908 when Mutt brought him home from an insane asylum. The strip is credited as the first continually published six-day weekly of American comics. It continued in abbreviated form as late as 1982.

1

2

3

4

5

6

7

8

9

1
MUTT & JEFF 8″ and 6.25″ tall clothed composition figures with ball-jointed body parts c. 1921.   EACH $250

2
JEFF 3″ tall painted bisque figure c. 1920s. $60

3
MUTT & JEFF 4″ and 3″ tall painted composition figures with spring-mounted noses c. 1920s.   EACH $75

4
MUTT 5.25″ tall china cream pitcher c. 1920s. $100

5
MUTT & JEFF 5.5″ tall silvered cast iron bank c. 1915. $150

6
"MUTT AND JEFF IN MEXICO" 4x9″ bwr cardboard ink blotter for musical stage comedy c. 1915. $15

7
"MUTT AND JEFF IN COLLEGE" 4x9″ bwr cardboard ink blotter for musical stage comedy c. 1915. $15

8
MUTT & JEFF 5.5x15″ cartoon book © 1910. $100

9
MUTT & JEFF 5.5x15″ cartoon book No. 4 © 1914. $125

10
MUTT & JEFF 11x16″ Cupples &
Leon book © 1920. $150

11
MUTT & JEFF 10x10″ Cupples &
Leon book © 1926. $100

12
MUTT & JEFF 10x10″ Cupples &
Leon book No. 14 © 1929. $50

13
MUTT & JEFF 10x10″ Cupples &
Leon book © 1933. $50

14
MUTT & JEFF 14x22″ bwr poster for
stage musical comedy c. 1915. $150

15
MUTT & JEFF 7x12″ rwb diecut
cardboard heads c. 1921. $50

16
"MUTT & JEFF AT THE RACES"
10x13.5″ sheet music with rwb cover
© 1921. $35

17
MUTT & JEFF 9x12″ souvenir album
from stage musical comedy
c. 1915. $35

18
MUTT & JEFF 10.5x14″ musical
comedy songbook © 1912. $40

19
"MUTT & JEFF IN PANAMA"
10x13.5″ sheet music © 1913. $40

20
MUTT & JEFF 3.5x5.5″ full color
postcard © 1909. $20

21
MUTT & JEFF 5x9x2.5″ tall wood cigar box c. 1920s. $60

22
"MUTT BRAND" 10x11″ full color
fruit crate label sticker c. 1930s. $50

23
JEFF 8x10″ bread premium mask
© 1933. $10

10

11

12   **13**   **14**

15

16

17

18   **19**   **20**

21   **22**   **23**

The Newlyweds

Creator: George McManus

Began: 1904. New York World, later Hearst and King Features Syndicates.

Principal Characters: Newlyweds, baby Snookums.

Synopsis: One of the several early strips created by McManus, based around parents named simply Mr. and Mrs. Newlywed and their ill-tempered infant, to be later named Snookums, known best for raucous crying and screaming fits. Strip was also known briefly in early years as *Their Only Child* and was revived for about 10 years beginning in 1944 under *Snookums* title.

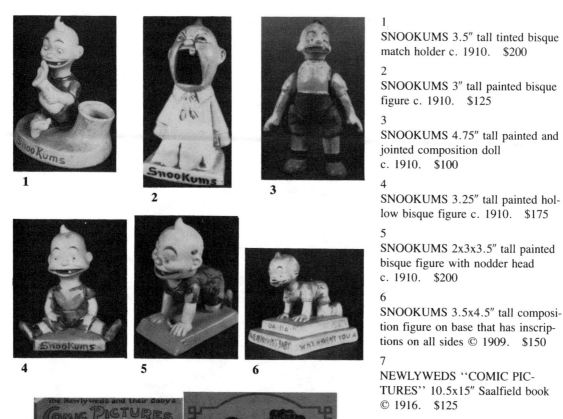

1

2

3

4

5

6

7

1
SNOOKUMS 3.5″ tall tinted bisque match holder c. 1910. $200

2
SNOOKUMS 3″ tall painted bisque figure c. 1910. $125

3
SNOOKUMS 4.75″ tall painted and jointed composition doll c. 1910. $100

4
SNOOKUMS 3.25″ tall painted hollow bisque figure c. 1910. $175

5
SNOOKUMS 2x3x3.5″ tall painted bisque figure with nodder head c. 1910. $200

6
SNOOKUMS 3.5x4.5″ tall composition figure on base that has inscriptions on all sides © 1909. $150

7
NEWLYWEDS "COMIC PICTURES" 10.5x15″ Saalfield book © 1916. $125

8
"THE NEWLYWEDS AND THEIR BABY" 10x13″ Saalfield book © 1907. $100

9
"THE NEWLYWED" 5x5x5″ tall full color tin candy box c. 1910. $500

8   9

Peanuts

Creator: Charles Schulz

Began: (D) 10/2/50; (S) 1/6/52. United Features Syndicate.

Principal Characters: Charlie Brown, Snoopy, Lucy, Linus, Schroeder, Peppermint Patty, Pigpen, Franklin.

Synopsis: Probably the world's most widely read comic strip, and the inspiration for a wealth of merchandise items, Peanuts began syndication under that title after two years as a *"Li'l Folks"* feature for the St. Paul (Minn.) Pioneer Press.

1
CHARLIE BROWN 9″ tall painted vinyl figure c. 1960s. $40

2
LINUS 9″ tall painted vinyl figure c. 1960s. $40

3
LUCY 9″ tall painted vinyl figure c. 1960s. $40

4
CHARLIE BROWN 6″ tall painted composition bobbing head figure c. 1960s. $50

5
SCHROEDER 5.5″ tall painted composition bobbing head figure c. 1960s. $50

6
LINUS 5.5″ tall painted composition bobbing head figure c. 1960s. $50

7
SNOOPY 6.5″ tall ceramic bank © 1968. $150

8
SNOOPY 7.5″ tall rubber squeeze toy © 1958. $40

9
SNOOPY 6″ tall vinyl squeaker toy © 1966. $15

10
SNOOPY wristwatch by Timex c. 1974. $50

11
LUCY wristwatch c. 1974. $60

12
"THE IN CROWD" 3″ diameter bwr celluloid button © 1966. $30

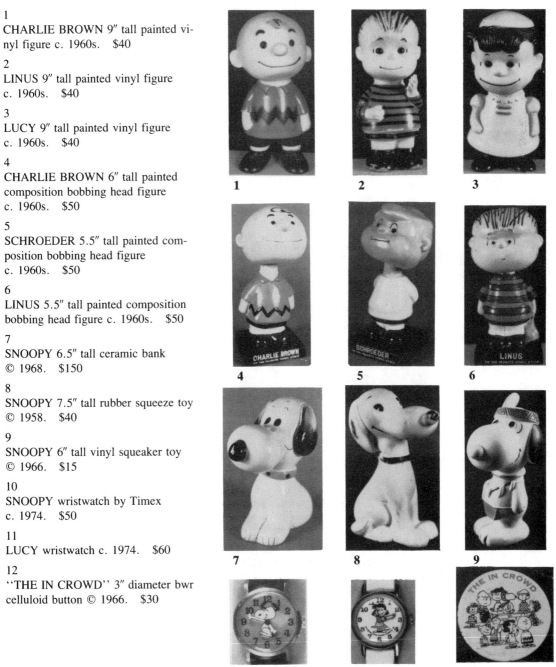

1   2   3

4   5   6

7   8   9

10   11   12

13

14

15

16

17

18

19

20

21

22

23

24

25

13
CHARLIE BROWN 5.5″ tall wood and full color composition music box by Anri of Italy c. 1968. $125

14
SNOOPY 4″ tall wood and full color composition music box by Anri of Italy c. 1968. $100

15
LINUS 5.5″ tall wood and full color composition music box by Anri of Italy © 1968. $125

16
CHARLIE BROWN 8″ tall composition figure with brass candleholder in hands by Hallmark c. 1970s. $20

17
LUCY 8″ tall composition figure with brass candleholder by Hallmark c. 1970s. $20

18
LINUS 7.5″ tall composition figure with brass candleholder inserted in blanket. By Hallmark c. 1970s. $20

19
SNOOPY ASTRONAUT 7.5″ tall vinyl doll in fabric uniform and clear plastic globe helmet. © 1969. $50

20
SNOOPY 5x5x5.5″ tall tin pop-up music box by Mattel © 1966. $30

21
SNOOPY "SPACE PATROL" 11″ long metal and plastic battery operated rocketship c. 1969. $150

22
SNOOPY CHEF 7.5″ tall plastic wind-up toy that flips a disk in the frying pan. c. 1970s. $30

23
SNOOPY 14″ tall plastic crank guitar by Mattel © 1970. $25

24
PEANUTS 10x19″ boxed board game by Selchow & Righter © 1959. $50

25
"LUCY'S TEA PARTY GAME" in 3.5x13x18″ wide box. By Milton Bradley © 1971. $35

26
PEANUTS 8.5x11″ coloring book by Saalfield © 1960. $40

27
"LIFE" 10.5x13.5″ magazine with Peanuts cover article. Issue for March 17, 1967. $12

28
"A BOY NAMED CHARLIE BROWN" 8.5x14″ pressbook for full-length movie © 1969. $40

29
PEANUTS 7x8.5x4″ deep flat steel lunch box by King-Seeley c. 1966. BOX $30, BOTTLE (NOT SHOWN) $15

30
SNOOPY 4.5x6.5x8.5″ long domed steel lunch box by King-Seeley © 1968.   BOX $45, BOTTLE (NOT SHOWN) $20

31
PEANUTS 7x9x4″ deep vinyl lunch box by King-Seeley © 1972.   BOX $40, BOTTLE (NOT SHOWN) $20

32
PEANUTS 7x8.5x4″ deep vinyl lunch box by King-Seeley c. late 1960s. BOX $35, BOTTLE (NOT SHOWN) $20

33
PEANUTS 7x9x4″ deep vinyl lunch box with steel bottle by King-Seeley c. 1971.   BOX $40, BOTTLE $20

34
PEANUTS 4x7.5x8.5″ tall vinyl zippered lunch box with carrying strap and plastic thermos by King-Seeley © 1965.   BAG $35, BOTTLE $15

35
PEANUTS tea set with 7x10″ tin tray and individual character tin saucers and plates 3″ to 5″ diameter. c. 1970s.   COMPLETE $50

26   **27**

28

29   **30**

31

32

33

34   **35**

Peter Rabbit

Creator: Harrison Cady

Began: (S) 8/15/20. New York Tribune.

Later Artists and/or Writers: Vincent Fago.

Principal Characters: Peter Rabbit, wife Hepsy, twin sons (both named Petey), Old Mr. Bear, Mr. Possum.

Synopsis: Strip based on characters by Cady from Thornton Burgess children's books, although the Rabbit family locale for the strip was changed to Carrotville, a typical middle class community. Adventures generally were about Peter's incessant botched attempts at meaningful community service. Strip characters included a host of animals, bugs, insects. The strip ceased in 1956.

1

1
PETER RABBIT 7x9″ cut-out book by Nourse Co. © 1916. $40

2
PETER RABBIT 5x8″ coloring and activity book from series c. 1930s. $30

3
PETER RABBIT 10x13″ Whitman paint book © 1937. $35

4
PETER RABBIT "STAND-UPS" 10.5x12.5″ Saalfield punch-out book © 1934. $60

5
PETER RABBIT "POP-UP" 4x5″ Blue Ribbon Press book © 1934. $60

6
PETER RABBIT 9.5x13″ Whitman picture storybook with Beatrix Potter story © 1936. $25

7
"PETER RABBIT CHILDREN'S STATIONERY" 1x6.25x9″ long boxed set of note sheets and envelopes. Picture shows box lid and example note sheet. c. 1930s. $40

8
"PETER RABBIT RING TOSS" 7.5x12″ boxed Milton Bradley target game c. 1930s. $50

9
"PETER RABBIT BABY POWDER" 4.25″ oval by 3.5″ tall full color tin container. Photo shows both sides. c. 1930s. $125

The Phantom

Creator: Lee Falk (writer), Ray Moore (artist)

Began: (D) 2/17/36; (S) 5/28/39. King Features Syndicate.

Later Artists and/or Writers: Wilson McCoy, Bill Lignante, Sy Barry.

Principal Characters: The Phantom, his wolf dog Devil, fiancee Diana Palmer, Pygmy leader Guran.

Synopsis: Mystic adventure strip about ''The Ghost Who Walks,'' a masked and purple-costumed fighter of evil. The Phantom is mortal, and is succeeded by a son each generation to carry on a tradition beginning at the time of Christopher Columbus. A movie version was released in 1943, and merchandise items began in the 1940s, still continuing to the present.

1
PHANTOM 5″ tall composition wood figure © 1944. $250

2
PHANTOM 5″ tall ceramic mug c. 1940s. $75

3
PHANTOM Whitman Big Little Book #1100 © 1936. $35

4
PHANTOM Whitman Better Little Book #1468 © 1945. $25

5
PHANTOM Whitman Better Little Book #1421 © 1941. $45

6
PHANTOM Whitman Better Little Book #1474 © 1939. $40

7
''THE SON OF THE PHANTOM'' 5.5x8″ Whitman book with dust jacket. © 1946. $30

8
PHANTOM 8.5x11.5″ Feature Book No. 20 comic book with first Phantom appearance in this series. © 1936. $255

9
PHANTOM 8.5x11.5″ Feature Book No. 22 comic book © 1936. $200

10
PHANTOM 1x6x11.25″ wide boxed set of parts for three games played on double-sided board. By Built-Rite © 1956. $75

11
PHANTOM 2x9x17.5″ wide boxed Transogram game © 1966. $125

1 2 3

4 5 6

7 8 9

10 11

Pogo

Creator: Walt Kelly

Began: 1949.

Later Artists and/or Writers: Selby Kelly, Stephen Kelly.

Principal Characters: Pogo Possum, Albert Alligator, Porky Pine, Beauregard Hound, Churchy la Femme (turtle), Howland Owl, P. T. Bridgeport (bear).

Synopsis: Creature fantasy and satire strip set in an Okefenokee swamp community. Pogo is generally the rational mediator of zany antics and events started by companion characters. The strip was discontinued in 1975.

1
POGO 2.75″ tall china figure made in Ireland © 1959. $300

2
POGO & FRIENDS 5.5″ tall or shorter set of six vinyl figures offered as soap box premiums by Procter & Gamble. © 1969.   EACH $12

3
POGO 5″ tall vinyl figure with artificial fur lower outfit. By Poynter Products © 1968. $150

4
HOWLAND OWL 5.5″ tall vinyl figure with artificial feathers. By Poynter Products © 1968. $150

5
BEAUREGARD HOUND 7″ tall vinyl figure with artificial fur ears. By Poynter Products © 1968. $150

6
CHURCHY LA FEMME 5.5″ tall vinyl figure with artificial fur neckpiece. By Poynter Products © 1968. $150

7
''CUE'' 8.5x11.5″ magazine for 8/25/56. $40

8
POGO Dell Comic #2 for April-June 1950. $135

9
''POGO'' 5x8″ first edition printing by Simon & Schuster © 1951. $50

10
''I GO POGO'' 5x8″ first edition printing by Simon & Schuster © 1952. $40

11
POGO 4.5x7″ Crest Book first edition paperback © 1964. $15

12
"I GO POGO" 4″ diameter large version orange/bw litho button © 1956. $75 (⅞″ SIZE FROM 1952 OR 1956, EACH $15)

13
"I GO POGO" 4.5x4.5″ packet holding set of three View-Master reels © 1980. $40

14
"SONGS OF THE POGO" 12x12″ record album by AA Records © 1956. $100

15
POGO 8.5x11.5″ Whitman coloring book © 1953. $100

16
POGO 8.25x11″ Treasure Book coloring book © 1964. Photo shows front cover and example page. $100

17
"POGO MOBILE" 10.5x13.5″ envelope holding 22 cardboard characters to form strung ceiling mobile c. 1960s. $200

18
WALT KELLY 4.25x5.5″ (closed) personal Christmas card shown opened in photo. © 1960. $100

19
WALT KELLY 4.25x5.5″ (closed) personal Christmas card shown opened in photo. © 1961. $100

20
ALBERT ALLIGATOR 5x6.5″ full color cartoon animation art on 10.5x12.5″ clear acetate sheet for M-G-M series c. 1970s. $300

21
POGO CHARACTER 4.25″ tall set of six plastic mugs c. late 1960s.   EACH $15

12 13 14

15 16

17

18

19

20 21

Popeye (Thimble Theatre)

Creator: E. C. Segar

Began: 1929. King Features Syndicate.

Later Artists and/or Writers: Bud Sagendorf, Tom Sims, Doc Winner, Bill Zaboly, Ralph Stein.

Principal Characters: Popeye, Olive Oyl, Wimpy, Swee'Pea, Jeep, many others in early version.

Synopsis: Originally begun in 1919 as *Thimble Theatre,* a parody of actual theatre productions, Popeye was introduced January 17, 1929 and rapidly displaced Harold Ham Gravy as the romantic interest for Olive. The awkwardly shaped Popeye the Sailor has remained one of the comics' best known and best merchandised characters to the present.

1

2

3

1
POPEYE 5″ tall painted and jointed wood figure. 1930s. $150

2
JEEP 4″ tall painted and jointed wood figure © 1936. $250

3
WIMPY 8″ tall painted plaster ashtray. 1930s. $125

4

5

4
POPEYE/WIMPY/OLIVE 3.25″ tall set of painted iron figurines © 1929.   EACH $100

5
"ASK POPEYE'S LUCKY JEEP" 1x5x7.5″ tall boxed cardboard mechanical game by Northwestern Products © 1936. $200

6

7

6
POPEYE & OLIVE "JIGGERS" 3.5x5x9.5″ tall full color tin wind-up toy by Marx © 1936.   BOXED $1500, LOOSE $1200

7
POPEYE PUNCHING BAG 3x5x6.5″ tall full color tin wind-up toy by J. Chein Co. 1930s. $1200

8
WIMPY 7″ tall celluloid jointed wind-up figure toy in box. 1930s.
BOXED $1000, LOOSE $800

9
POPEYE WITH PARROT CAGES 8.5″ tall full color tin wind-up walking toy by Marx © 1932. $300

10
"POPEYE THE PILOT" 6″ long full color tin wind-up toy by Marx © 1940.   VARIETY SHOWN $400, EARLIER VERSION WITH COLOR AROUND NECK AND "47" ON SIDE OF PLANE $500

8

9

10

11
POPEYE TANK 4″ long full color tin
wind-up toy by Linemar
c. 1960s. $300

12
"POPEYE TRANSIT CO." 13.5″
long full color tin friction truck by Linemar c. 1960s. $500

13
POPEYE 10x10″ Series 1 daily strip
reprint book by Sonnet Co.
© 1931. $150

14
POPEYE 10x10″ Series 2 comic strip
reprint book by Sonnet Co.
© 1932. $125

15
POPEYE 10x10″ book No. 1 by
David McKay © 1935. $100

16
POPEYE 8.5x11″ Whitman Big Big
Book © 1935. $100

17
POPEYE & JEEP 8.5x11.5″ Feature
Book No. 3 comic © 1936. $260

18
POPEYE 8x9″ Whitman book
© 1937. $40

19
POPEYE 8x13″ cartoon book by Saalfield © 1934. $250

20
POPEYE 10x14.5″ paint book by
McLoughlin © 1937. $100

21
POPEYE 8.5x10.5″ book of cartoon
drawing instructions by David McKay
Co. © 1939. $30

22
POPEYE 7x9″ school composition
tablet © 1929. $30

23
"I'M POPEYE THE SAILOR MAN"
10x12.5″ sheet music © 1934. $25

24
POPEYE SUNSHINE BISCUITS
1.5x3x5.5″ long full color box
© 1935. Photo shows two of five illustrated panels. $200

11

12

13

14

15

16

17

18

19

20

21

22

23

24

25

26

27

28

29

30

31

32   **33**   **34**

35

25
POPEYE CLUB 3.5x4.25″ bw membership card. 1930s. $75

26
''DRINK POPEYE'' (cola) colorful diecut cardboard store sign about 24″ tall © 1929. $300

27
POPEYE ORIGINAL STRIP ART on 16.5x22.5″ white sheet inked in black by Bud Sagendorf for publication Sunday, Nov. 9, 1975. $115

28
POPEYE ORIGINAL STRIP ART on 6x17.5″ white sheet inked in black by Bud Sagendorf for daily strip of May 31, 1976. $100

29
POPEYE 3½″ rwb celluloid button c. 1950s. $35

30
JEEP 13/16″ full color litho tin button © 1936. $40

31
POPEYE wristwatch with small Wimpy animated inset by New Haven Time Co. © 1935. $300

32
POPEYE pocketwatch with small Wimpy animated inset by New Haven Time Co. © 1934. $450

33
POPEYE 1.5x4.5″ diameter metal wind-up clock with animated Swee'pea figure. By Smiths of England © 1967. $150

34
POPEYE .75x2.5x2.5″ rwb/silver tin dime register bank © 1929. $75

35
''POPEYE-CHEERS'' 2.5x5.5x9.5″ long box holding set of eight plastic Christmas bulb shades.
© 1929.   BOXED $250, LOOSE SHADES EACH $15

36
"POPEYE PIPE TOSS GAME" in
1x4.5x9.5″ tall box by Rosebud Art
© 1935. $75

37
"POPEYE RING TOSS GAME" in
2x10.5x15.5″ wide box
© 1933. $125

38
POPEYE 1.5x11x22″ wide boxed
tiddly-wink game by Parker Brothers
© 1948. $150

39
POPEYE 1x3.5x7″ tall boxed set of
glass marbles and leather pouch.
© 1929. $150

40
POPEYE 1x6x9″ wide cardboard pencil box © 1929. $50

41
POPEYE 1x5x6.5″ tall boxed Whitman card game © 1934. $40

42
"POPEYE PAINT-O-GRAF"
2x17x17″ boxed Milton Bradley mechanical drawing set. Photo shows lid
and contents. © 1935. $100

43
"POPEYE'S NAILING SET"
1.5x9.5x13″ wide boxed kit of toy
tools by Bar Zim Co. © 1934. $100

44
"POPEYE'S BIG BAND" 2x12x19″
wide boxed set of toy instruments
© 1933. $100

45
POPEYE 5″ long wood battery operated pipe on 5.5x9″ card
© 1958. $50

46
"POPEYE BUBBLE-SET" in
2x5x7.5″ wide box by Transogram
© 1936. $50

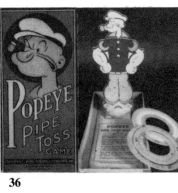

36

37

38

39

40

41   **42**

43

44

45

46

Prince Valiant

Creator: Harold Foster

Began: (S) 2/14/37. United Features Syndicate.

Later Artists and/or Writers: John Cullen Murphy, Cullen Murphy.

Principal Characters: Prince Valiant, wife Aleta, son Prince Arn, Sir Gawain.

Synopsis: Re-creation of King Arthur days featuring courageous self-taught knight-warrior Prince Valiant. A strip noted for its precision art and attention to historic detail and authenticity, Prince Valiant has been continued since the early 1970s by John Cullen Murphy and son. A 1953 movie starred Robert Wagner and Janet Leigh as Aleta.

1
PRINCE VALIANT 5″ tall composition wood figure © 1944. $150

2
PRINCE VALIANT 7x10″ book with dust jacket by Hastings House © 1951. $30

3
PRINCE VALIANT 7x10″ book with dust jacket by Hastings House © 1952. $30

4
PRINCE VALIANT 7x10″ book with dust jacket by Hastings House © 1953. $35

5
PRINCE VALIANT 7x10″ book with dust jacket by Hastings House © 1956. $35

6
PRINCE VALIANT 7x10″ book with dust jacket by Hastings House © 1960. $35

7
PRINCE VALIANT 6.5x8″ Treasure Book © 1954. $15

8
PRINCE VALIANT 11x14″ Saalfield coloring book © 1954. $30

9
PRINCE VALIANT/PRINCESS ALETA 10x14″ Saalfield doll book © 1954. $100

10
"PRINCE VALIANT ARCHERY SET" in 2x3.5x48″ long box c. 1950s. $75

11

12

13

14

15   **16**

17   **18**

19

11
PRINCE VALIANT 9x10″ erasable crayon book © 1955. $25

12
PRINCE VALIANT 2x6.5x8″ boxed jigsaw puzzle by Built-Rite
c. 1950s. $40

13
"THE YOUNG KNIGHT" 8x11″ book with Hal Foster art for "Young Arn" story. © 1945. $40

14
PRINCE VALIANT "CASTLE FORT" 4x9x26″ wide boxed Marx playset c. 1950s.   COMPLETE $300

15
PRINCE VALIANT 1x10x10″ boxed "Crossbow Pistol Game"
© 1948. $75

16
PRINCE VALIANT .75x2.5x2.5″ tin dime register bank © 1954. $100

17
PRINCE VALIANT 2x10.5x19″ tall boxed set of battle toys
c. 1950s. $100

18
PRINCE VALIANT 4.5x13.5″ retail pack holding 9″ tall diecut vinyl magnetic figure. © 1975. $10

19
PRINCE VALIANT 2x9x17.5″ wide boxed game by Transogram. Photo shows box lid plus contents detail. Mid-1950s. $60

Red Ryder

Creator: Fred Harman

Began: (S) 11/6/38; (D) 3/27/39. Newspaper Enterprise Assn.

Later Artists and/or Writers: Bob McLeod.

Principal Characters: Red Ryder, Little Beaver.

Synopsis: Probably the most popular western strip, it resulted in many film versions and a radio show in the 1940s as well as other print media. During this era, the fictictious Red Ryder supplanted living cowboy star Buck Jones as the symbol figure of Daisy Mfg. Co., maker of air rifle toys so popular at the time. His youthful Indian sidekick, Little Beaver, remained faithful and, apparently the same age, from the strip's outset until its cessation in late 1960s.

1

2

3

1
RED RYDER Whitman Better Little Book #1440 © 1940. $25

2
RED RYDER Whitman Better Little Book #1466 © 1949. $20

3
RED RYDER 3x4″ Whitman Penny Book © 1939. $30

4
RED RYDER 4x5.5″ Fast-Action Story book c. mid-1940s. $40

5
RED RYDER 5.5x8″ Whitman book with dust jacket © 1946. $20

6
RED RYDER/LITTLE BEAVER 8.5x11.5″ Whitman paint book © 1947. $25

4   5

6

7
"DAISY HANDBOOK NO. 2" 4.5x5.25″ catalog and comic manual by Daisy Mfg. Co. including Red Ryder air rifle ads. © 1948. $60

8
RED RYDER 6.5″ diameter picture record by Record Guild Of America © 1948. $40

9
"RED RYDER GUN BOOK" 4.5x5.25″ catalog manual by Daisy Mfg. Co. with air rifle ads. © 1955. $75

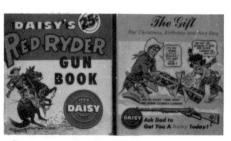

7

8

10
RED RYDER 8.5x11″ bw radio time announcement card by N.B.C. Bread. 1940s. $125

9

10

11

12

13

14

15

16

17

18

19

20

11
RED RYDER/LITTLE BEAVER
3.5x5.5″ bw fan card c. late
1940s. $50

12
"RIDE, RYDER, RIDE!" 22x28″
half-sheet full color movie poster
© 1948. $30

13
RED RYDER ORIGINAL STRIP
ART on 7x23″ white sheet inked in
black by Fred Harman for daily newspaper strip of Sept. 5, 1957. $150

14
"RED RYDER VICTORY PATROL"
6.5x15″ rwb paper sign by bread
sponsor. $200

15
RED RYDER 3″ diameter paper Radio
Decoder from Victory Patrol kit
c. early 1940s. $100

16
RED RYDER 2.25x3″ rwb member
card for Victory Patrol dated
1943. $50

17
"RED RYDER TARGET GAME"
1.5x10x13″ tall boxed Whitman set
© 1939. $100

18
RED RYDER 1x6x11″ wide boxed
three-game set by Built-Rite
© 1956. $35

19
RED RYDER 3.5x11.5x15.5″ wide
metal and cardboard salesman's case
for glove lines of Wells-Lamont Co.
c. late 1940s-early 1950s. $200

20
RED RYDER "Trigger Mitt" fabric
glove set by Wells-Lamont Co. on
6x10″ trading card sheet © 1952.
GLOVES $30, UNCUT CARDS $75

Roy Rogers

Creator: Al McKimson

Began: (D) 12/2/49; (S) 12/4/49. King Features Syndicate.

Principal Characters: Roy Rogers, Trigger, Dale Evans, Gabby Hayes, Pat Brady.

Synopsis: Adventure strip which paralleled the cowboy achievements in many earlier films and books by ''The King of the Cowboys'' and Trigger, ''The Smartest Horse in the Movies.'' Countless merchandise items, prompted also by the 1950s television series, appeared in that decade. Newspaper publication ceased in 1961.

1

2

3

4

5

6   7   8

9

1
ROY ROGERS 8x10″ full color Dixie Ice Cream picture. 1940s. $40

2
ROY ROGERS 8x10″ full color Dixie Ice Cream picture.   1940s. $30

3
''ROY ROGERS TRICK LASSO'' 14.5x24″ cardboard store display with actual rope lasso over wire mounted at center. 1950s. $800

4
ROY ''SOUVENIR CUP'' 15x22″ poster sheet by Quaker Oats for premium cup (see next item) with July 1950 date. $400

5
ROY 4x4x4″ tall plastic Quaker Oats premium cup. Early 1950s. $25

6
ROY ROGERS 6.5″ tall full color painted composition bobbing head figure c. 1950s. $115

7
ROY & TRIGGER 8.5″ tall (excluding bulb socket) full color painted plaster lamp with 5.5″ tall cardboard shade. 1950s.   COMPLETE $250, NO SHADE $175

8
ROY & TRIGGER 7x10″ card holding 4″ Hartland Plastics figure set c. late 1950s-early 1960s. $75

9
ROY STAGECOACH TRAIN 2x2.5x14″ long tin and plastic Marx wind-up toy 1950s. $250

10

"TRIGGER" 12x26x18" tall wood
and metal toy rocking horse
c. 1950s. $125

11

ROY 3.5x4.5x15.5" long box containing Marx metal vehicle and plastic
figure set c. 1950s.   BOXED $300,
NO BOX $200

12

ROY 3x8x21" long boxed "Rodeo
Ranch" playset by Marx c. 1950s.
COMPLETE $300

13

ROY 8.5x11" cardboard announcement sign for start of daily comic strip
January 2, 1950. $150

14

ROY 5.5x8.25" announcement booklet
for movie and start of daily comic
strip early 1950. $100

15

ROY ORIGINAL COMIC ART
5.5x17.5" white art sheet in black ink
by Arens for daily newspaper publication July 16, 1959. $150

16

ROY 8.5x11" Whitman paint book
© 1944. $50

17

EARLY ROY 11.5x15.5" publicity
newspaper for New York appearance
July 16, 1938. $75

18

ROY 8.5x11" rodeo tour souvenir program c. 1950. $40

19

ROY 10.5x13" Whitman paperdoll
book © 1948. $150

20

ROY & DALE 10x12" Whitman paperdoll album © 1954. $75

21

ROY/DODGE CITY 5x8" comic book
for Dodge cars © 1955. $40

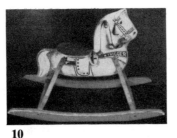

10

11

12

13

14

15

16

17

18

19

20   **21**

22

23

24

25

26

27

28

29

30

31

32

33

22
"TV DIGEST" 5.5x8" issue for week of March 1, 1952 with Roy cover article. $50

23
ROY 2.75" blw Dixie Ice Cream lid c. 1940s. $15

24
POST CEREAL 2.5x3.25" "Pop-Out" punch-out 3-D card from set of 36 issued 1953-1955.   EACH UNPUNCHED $15

25
ROY 4x8" paper pop gun for "Roy Rogers Cookies" c. mid-1950s. $35

26
ROY 2x11.5x15.5" wide boxed oil painting set by Avalon c. mid-1950s. $150

27
ROY RODEO 10.5x12" RCA Victor record album © 1950. $50

28
ROY/PECOS BILL 10.5x12" RCA Victor record album c. 1948. $50

29
ROY ON TRIGGER wristwatch by Ingraham c. 1951. $150

30
ROY & TRIGGER 11x14" tray puzzle by Watkins-Strathmore c. early 1950s. $20

31
ROY 11x14" Whitman tray puzzle © 1952. $20

32
ROY ON TRIGGER 2x5x5" metal animated wind-up alarm clock in two versions with and without "Roy Rogers" name on dial face. By Ingraham c. 1951.   WITH NAME $175, WITHOUT NAME $125

33
ROY "QUICK SHOOTER" black felt hat with pop-out Derringer miniature cap pistol in 5x10x12" wide box by Ideal c. mid-1950s.   BOXED $150, LOOSE $100

34
ROY & TRIGGER 3x3.25x4″ tall black metal and plastic snapshot camera with silvered metal title plate. By Herbert George Co. c. late 1940s. $75

35
"ROY ROGERS DEPUTY" 2.5″ bronze finished embossed tin badge c. 1950. $20

36
ROY & TRIGGER 2x4x4.5″ wide black plastic and metal binoculars. 1950s. $50

37
ROY 1x7x14″ wide boxed set of four hard rubber horseshoes and two tin target bases with peg for each. 1950s. $125

38
ROY 6.5″ long metal battery operated "Signal Gun" in box. 1950s. BOXED $200, LOOSE $125

39
ROY & TRIGGER 8″ long child's fabric necktie c. 1950s. $50

40
ROY "DOUBLE R BAR RANCH" child's T-shirt. 1950s. $75

41
ROY 3″ tall china mug c. early 1950s. $50

42
ROY 4.25″ long plastic and metal harmonica on 4.5x6″ card. 1950s. $50

43
ROY & DALE 4x14x24″ wide boxed plastic "Western Dinner Set" by Ideal © 1958. $75

44
ROY 7x9x4″ deep tan vinyl "Saddlebag" lunch box with 8″ steel bottle by King-Seeley c. 1960. BOX $150, BOTTLE $40

45
ROY "MAGIC PLAY AROUND" 5x10x15″ tall boxed set of cardboard punch-out buildings and figures by Amsco. 1950s. $150

34

35

36

37

38

39

40

41

42

43

44

45

The Shadow

Creator: Vernon Greene

Began: 1938. Ledger Syndicate.

Principal Characters: The Shadow (Lamont Cranston), girlfriend Margo Lane.

Synopsis: Short-lived strip although faithful in style to The Shadow character created by Maxwell Grant (pen name for Walter B. Gibson) for Street & Smith pulp magazines in the early 1930s. Also a popular 1930s radio show, The Shadow has re-emerged sporadically through the 1980s, usually in comic book form. Newspaper publication ceased in 1942.

1
THE SHADOW Whitman Better Little Book #1430 © 1940. $100

2
THE SHADOW Whitman Better Little Book #1443 © 1941. $60

3
THE SHADOW 5x7.5″ book by Ideal Library © 1931. $100

4
THE SHADOW 5x7.5″ book by Street & Smith © 1931. $80

5
THE SHADOW 3x4″ bwr paper ad sticker for pulp magazine. 1930s. $150

6
THE SHADOW 11x14″ ad poster for radio broadcasts. 1930s. $350

7
THE SHADOW 7x10″ pulp magazine for November 1, 1933. $75

8
THE SHADOW 8.5x11.5″ annual pulp edition for 1942. $75

9
THE SHADOW 6x7″ opened folder card for radio broadcasts in 3x6″ envelope, not shown. 1930s. $75

10
THE SHADOW 8x10″ bw photo premium from radio sponsor "blue coal." 1930s. $150

11
THE SHADOW 3x5.5″ card which held emblem lapel stud premium pictured on card. 1930s.   CARD $250, WITH STUD $450

12
THE SHADOW 3x4.5″ instruction
sheet for "blue coal" premium glow
ring in mailing envelope.
1930s. $250

13
THE SHADOW 1″ luminous white
plastic 'blue coal' ring with simulated
blue plastic coal piece mounted on
top. 1930s. $300

14
THE SHADOW 4x9″ cardboard ink
blotter by radio sponsor "blue coal"
c. early 1940s. $60

15
THE SHADOW 1.5x4″ opened
matchbook cover by radio sponsor
"blue coal." Photo shows outside and
inside of single cover. c. early
1940s. $100

16
THE SHADOW 13.5x15″ brown felt
hat with "The Shadow" imprint on
inside liner. c. early 1940s. $300

17
THE SHADOW 1.5x10.5x20.5″ wide
boxed game by Toy Creation. Photo
shows box lid and playing board.
© 1940. $500

18
THE SHADOW 4.5″ long plastic jet
aircraft toy in 2.5x6x6″ blister pack
© 1977.   PACKAGED $50, LOOSE
$25

19
THE SHADOW 3.5x4.5x11.5″ long
plastic battery operated "Crime
Fighter" helicopter c. 1970s. $35

20
THE SHADOW 3x8x11″ tall boxed
costume and plastic mask by College-
ville. Photo shows box, mask, costume chest art. © 1973. $35

12

13　　　**14**

15　　　**16**

17

18　　　**19**

20

Skippy

Creator: Percy Crosby

Began: (D) 6/23/25 (Johnson Features); (S) 10/17/26 (King Features Syndicate).

Principal Characters: Skippy Skinner, pals Sidney Saunders, Sooky Wayne.

Synopsis: Popular child character created in 1923, a mischievous, cynical, philosophic youngster always portrayed in the same checkered hat, large jacket, short trousers and floppy socks. The character inspired a 1930 Jackie Cooper movie plus a radio show beginning the following year. The strip ceased with Crosby's death in 1943.

1
SKIPPY 5.5″ tall painted bisque figure with movable arms. 1930s. $75

2
SKIPPY 7.5x9.5″ Whitman Big Big Book © 1934. $60

3
SKIPPY Whitman Big Little Book offered as premium by Phillips Magnesia Toothpaste © 1934. $35

4
SKIPPY Whitman Big Little Book #761 © 1934. $25

5
SKIPPY 8.5x11″ book © 1925. $40

6
SKIPPY/JACKIE COOPER 9x12″ sheet music from Paramount film © 1930. $40

7
SKIPPY 8x9.5″ ''Good Eyesight Brigade'' manual based on use of eyeglasses © 1937. $15

8
SKIPPY 2.25x3.25″ card from numbered set of 12 packed in Wheaties boxes c. 1933.   EACH $6

9
SKIPPY 24x36″ diecut cardboard store sign for ''Fro-Joy'' Ice Cream. 1930s. $75

10
SKIPPY 4.5x6″ Christmas card with personalized greeting at bottom inked by Percy Crosby. © 1931. $75

11
SKIPPY 8x10″ paper mask premium by Socony Oil. 1930s. $30

12
SKIPPY 1¼″ lithographed tin newspaper button. 1930s. $20

13
SKIPPY 2x10.5x14.5″ wide boxed
Milton Bradley game. Photo shows
lid, character pieces, 2/3 playing
board. © 1932. $150

14
SKIPPY 1x4x5″ wide boxed card
game by All-Fair. Photo shows lid
and example card. 1930s. $50

15
SKIPPY 2x12.5x17″ wide boxed paint
and coloring set by American Toy
Works © 1935. $40

16
SKIPPY 1x7x10.5″ wide boxed set of
three jigsaw puzzles © 1933. $30

17
SKIPPY 1x6x11″ wide cardboard pencil case © 1933. $25

18
SKIPPY 5.5″ tall diecut and woven
felt patch. 1930s. $35

19
SKIPPY 3x6″ ''Mystic Circle Club''
folder with order sheet for compass.
1930s. $60

20
SKIPPY .5x3x4″ tall box holding set
of crayon chalk sticks © 1935. $12

21
SKIPPY 17″ wide by 25″ tall by 33″
long steel tricycle with rubber tires.
Photo shows title decal with the toy.
1930s. $300

13

14

15

16

17

18

19

20

21

Smilin' Jack

Creator: Zack Mosley

Began: (S) 10/1/33; (D) 6/15/36. Chicago Tribune–New York News Syndicate.

Principal Characters: Smilin' Jack (Martin), Fat Stuff, Downwind, Cindy, Gale, Dixie, Joy, various other romantic interests.

Synopsis: Aviation-based adventure strip originally titled *On The Wing* featuring debonair pilot with an affinity for romantic adventures. The strip ceased in 1973.

1
SMILIN' JACK 5x6.5″ card with bw art plus photo of Zack Mosley with personalized inscription by him. Late 1930s-early 1940s. $85

2
SMILIN' JACK Whitman Better Little Book #1445 © 1943. $30

3
SMILIN' JACK Whitman Better Little Book #1473 © 1939. $30

4
SMILIN' JACK ORIGINAL ART 7.5x21″ white sheet inked in black by Zack Mosley for daily newspaper publication January 31, 1955. $125

5
SMILIN' JACK 2.5x3.75″ Whitman Penny Book © 1938. $18

6
SMILIN' JACK 3.5x3.5″ Whitman Top-Line Comic © 1935. $30

7
SMILIN' JACK 8.5x11″ Saalfield coloring book © 1946. $30

8
SMILIN' JACK 5.5x8″ Whitman book with dust jacket © 1942. $15

9
SMILIN' JACK Dell Series 1 issue #5 comic book © 1941. $260

10
SMILIN' JACK 7x10″ ''Popped Wheat'' cereal premium comic book © 1938 but probably early 1940s. $10

11
SMILIN' JACK 2.75x3″ bw strip cards of numbered set 1-128 from movie serial of 1943.   EACH $1

Smitty

Creator: Walter Berndt

Began: (D) 11/27/22; (S) 2/25/23. Chicago Tribune–New York News Syndicate.

Principal Characters: Smitty, Herby, Mr. Bailey, dog Spot.

Synopsis: Long-running strip about a prototype office boy (Augustus Smith) and his usually benevolent boss, Mr. Bailey. Smitty's younger brother, Herby, also was prominent in the strip. A companion strip about Herby was also syndicated circa 1930. Both strips ceased in 1973.

1
SMITTY 3.5″ tall painted bisque figure with nodder head. 1930s. $75

2
HERBY 2.25″ tall painted bisque figure with nodder head. 1930s. $75

3
SMITTY 13.5″ tall cloth doll. 1930s. $50

4
HERBY 11.5″ tall cloth doll. 1930s. $50

5
SMITTY Whitman Big Little Book issued as Cocomalt premium © 1934. $30

6
SMITTY Whitman Big Little Book #1477. 1930s. $30

7
SMITTY 7x8.5″ Cupples & Leon book © 1928. $20

8
SMITTY ORIGINAL ART 7x21″ white art sheet inked in black by Walter Berndt for daily newspaper publication August 28, 1931. $100

9
SMITTY/HERBY "TOOTSIETOY" 2.5″ long painted metal motorcycle and sidecar. 1930s. $250

10
SMITTY 1x8.5x16.5″ wide boxed Milton Bradley game. 1930s. $75

11
SMITTY 2x9x12″ wide boxed Milton Bradley target game. 1930s. $75

12
SMITTY wristwatch by New Haven Clock Co. c. 1935. $150

13
SMITTY 10x10″ McLoughlin Bros. coloring book © 1931. $30

Snuffy Smith

Creator: Billy DeBeck

Began: Mid-1930s. King Features Syndicate.

Later Artists and/or Writers: Fred Lasswell.

Principal Characters: Snuffy Smith, wife Lowizie, Jughaid.

Synopsis: Hillbilly character strip that evolved from Barney Google strip by DeBeck. Snuffy was introduced in 1934 and by the end of the decade his name was added to the Google strip title. By the mid-1940s, the Google name was dropped. The strip was continued by Fred Lasswell following DeBeck's death in 1942.

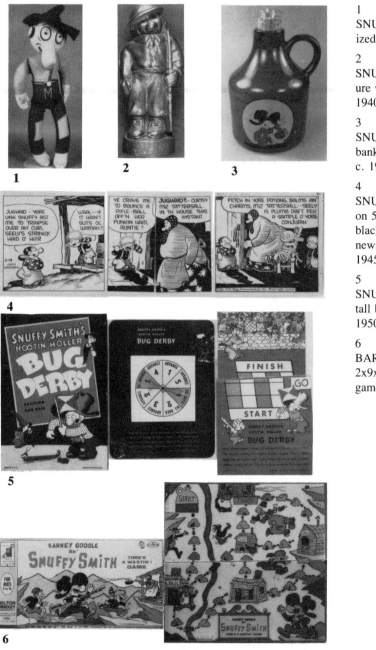

1
SNUFFY 17″ tall probably unauthorized felt doll. 1930s. $150

2
SNUFFY 4.75″ tall metal soldier figure with brass finish. Early 1940s. $50

3
SNUFFY 8″ tall ceramic whiskey jug bank with corncob stopper c. 1950s. $35

4
SNUFFY SMITH ORIGINAL ART on 5x15″ white art sheet inked in black by Fred Lasswell for daily newspaper publication Nov. 19, 1945. $75

5
SNUFFY "BUG DERBY" 1x7x10″ tall boxed Jaymar game c. early 1950s. $50

6
BARNEY GOOGLE/SNUFFY 2x9x16″ wide boxed Milton Bradley game © 1963. $40

Steve Canyon

Creator: Milton Caniff

Began: (D) 1/13/47; (S) 1/19/47. Field Newspaper Syndicate.

Later Artists and/or Writers: Ray Bailey, Dick Rockwell.

Principal Characters: Steve Canyon, Copper Calhoun, Poteet Canyon, Summer.

Synopsis: Last of the Caniff adventure strips about the globe-trotting intrigue missions of Canyon, a retired Air Force officer at the strip's outset. Canyon's missions often involved encounters with exotic females prior to his marriage to Summer in 1970. A TV series of 1958-59 was responsible for an assortment of merchandise items. Newspaper publication ceased in 1988.

1
STEVE CANYON 5.5x8″ book with dust jacket. © 1959. $12

2
STEVE CANYON 11x14″ coloring book © 1952. $25

3
STEVE CANYON 6.5x9″ comic strip book © 1957. $25

4
STEVE CANYON 8.5x8.5x9″ tall plastic "Jet Helmet" in box by Ideal © 1959.   BOXED $100, LOOSE $50

5
STEVE CANYON 2x10x20″ wide boxed game by Lowell Toy © 1959. $60

6
STEVE CANYON 5.5x6.5x24.5″ wide plastic "Glider Bomb" launch vehicle in box by Ideal © 1958. BOXED $125, LOOSE $75

7
STEVE CANYON 7x8x4″ deep steel lunch box. Photo shows front and inside front. By Aladdin © 1959. BOX $150, BOTTLE (NOT SHOWN) $50

1

2

3

4

5

6

7

Superman

Creator: Jerry Siegel (writer), Joe Shuster (artist)

Began: (D) 1/16/39; (S) 11/5/39. McClure Syndicate.

Principal Characters: Superman (alter ego Clark Kent), Lois Lane, Daily Planet editor Perry White, Jimmy Olsen.

Synopsis: Classic superhero first introduced in 1938 through first issue of Action Comics. Subsequent years produced an immensely popular radio show of the early 1940s plus several animated and live action films, the latest in 1983 (Superman III). Newspaper publication ceased in 1967.

1

2

3

1
FIRST "SUPERMAN" COMIC BOOK Summer Issue, 1939.   IF NEAR MINT $50,000

2
SECOND "SUPERMAN" COMIC BOOK Fall Issue, 1939. $3000

3
"SUPERMEN OF AMERICA—ACTION COMICS" 5.5″ diameter fabric premium patch from 1939. $1200

4
SUPERMAN 13″ tall jointed wood and composition doll with cloth cape. 1940s. $750

5
SUPERMAN 5.75″ tall composition wood figure c. 1944. $1500

6
SUPERMAN 15″ tall painted plaster carnival statue c. 1940s. $150

7
SUPERMAN 9.5″ tall painted china bank © 1949. $400

8
SUPERMAN 6x6″ plastic squirt gun c. 1966. $35

9
SUPERMAN "SOAKY" 10″ tall soap bottle © 1965. $25

10
SUPERMAN 11″ tall hand puppet with fabric body and vinyl head. By Ideal © 1966. $35

11
SUPERMAN 48″ tall pogo stick topped by vinyl torso figure. © 1977. $40

4

5

6

7

8

9

10

11

12
SUPERMAN 2.5x3x4″ long tin wind-
up turnover tank toy by Marx
© 1940. $500

13
SUPERMAN 11x15″ Saalfield coloring book © 1940. $150

14
SUPERMAN 11x15″ Saalfield coloring book © 1940. $100

15
SUPERMAN 11x15″ Saalfield coloring book © 1941. $75

16
SUPERMAN 8x11″ Whitman coloring
book © 1966. $25

17
SUPERMAN 6.5x9″ book by George
Lowther published by Random House
© 1942.   WITH DUST JACKET
$300, WITHOUT $150

18
SUPERMAN 10.5x14″ Saalfield cut-
out book © 1940. $400

19
"SUPERMEN OF AMERICA"
8.5x11″ membership certificate.
1948. $75

20
SUPERMAN 4x5″ Christmas card
c. early 1940s. $35

21
SUPERMAN 4x5″ Christmas card
c. early 1940s. $35

22
SUPERMAN 4.5x6″ waxed paper
wrapper from set of 72 cards by Gum,
Inc. © 1940. $300

23
SUPERMAN 2.5x3.25″ card #4 from
set of 72 by Gum, Inc. © 1940.
CARDS 1-48 EACH $12,
49-72 EACH $30

12

13   **14**   **15**

16   **17**   **18**

19   **20**   **21**

22   **23**

24

25

24
"SUPERMAN-TIM" 5x7″ monthly premium magazine from stores handling this merchandise line. Mid-1940s and pictured example is for March 1946. $20

25 "SUPERMAN TIES" 1x6.5x11″ tall boxed set. 1940s.   BOXED $250, LOOSE SINGLE TIE $75

26

27

26
SUPERMAN 1x8x10.5″ tall boxed set of two jigsaw puzzles © 1940. $150

27
SUPERMAN .5x2.5x2.5″ tin dime register bank. 1940s. $125

28
SUPERMAN 2x8x10″ tall boxed "Krypto-Ray Gun" film projector gun with films by Daisy Mfg. Co. 1940s.   BOXED $400, GUN ONLY $150

28

29

29
SUPERMAN wristwatch by New Haven Clock Co. 1939. $150

30
SUPERMAN 1.5x4x6.5″ wide boxed set of hand viewer and six boxed films © 1947. $150

31
SUPERMAN 1.5x4x6.5″ wide boxed set of hand viewer and two films by Acme © 1947. $150

30

31

32
SUPERMAN 1x9x11″ wide boxed paint set by American Toy Works. 1940s. $200

33
SUPERMAN 2x12x16″ wide boxed paint set by American Toy Works. 1940s. $200

32

33

34
SUPERMAN 1x10x12″ wide boxed crayon by number set by Transogram © 1954. $100

35
SUPERMAN 2x8x13″ wide boxed horseshoe set. 1950s. $100

34

35

36
"FLYING SUPERMAN" 5″ tall by
6.5″ wide plastic premium by Kellogg's with instruction sheet and
mailer. 1950s. COMPLETE $300,
TOY ONLY $200

37
"CALLING SUPERMAN" 2x9x17″
wide boxed Transogram game.
1950s. $75

38
SUPERMAN 2″ tall by 5″ diameter
white glass cereal bowl. 1950s. $100

39
SUPERMAN "MUSCLE BUILD-
ING" 2x11x18″ wide boxed set in-
cluding club button. 1954.
COMPLETE $250, WITHOUT
BUTTON $150

40
SUPERMAN "DINGLE-DANDY"
6x8″ assembled diecut cardboard ceiling mobile figure by Kellogg's.
1950s. $75

41
"FLYING SUPERMAN" 12.5″ tall
Transogram toy on 9x13″ card.
1950s. $150

42
"SUPERMAN CLUB" 3½″ celluloid
button © 1966. $20

43
SUPERMAN 1x9x14″ wide boxed battery operated quiz game. 1960s. $50

44
SUPERMAN 6.5x8.5x4″ deep steel
lunch box and bottle by King-Seeley
© 1967. BOX $150, BOTTLE $40

36

37 **38**

39

40

41

42 **43**

44

Tarzan

Creator: Edgar Rice Burroughs

Began: (D) 1/7/29 (Metropolitan Newspaper Service); (S) 3/15/31 (United Features Syndicate).

Principal Character: Tarzan.

Synopsis: Enduring ape-man character created by Burroughs circa 1912, done originally in comic strip form by Hal Foster and Rex Maxon and then followed by a host of succeeding artists and writers through the early 1980s. Tarzan also was heavily popularized between the 1930s and 1980s by movie versions, books, comic books.

1
TARZAN 7x9″ Book No. 1 by Grosset & Dunlap © 1929. $150

2
''TARZAN TWINS'' 6.5x8.5″ book by Volland Co. © 1927. $200

3
TARZAN Whitman Big Little Cartoon Book #744 © 1933. $100

4
TARZAN 5x5.5″ Whitman Big Little Book #1180 © 1935. $75

5
TARZAN Whitman Big Little Book #769 © 1934. $75

6
TARZAN Whitman Big Little Book #779 © 1934. $75

7
TARZAN TWINS Whitman Big Little Book #770 © 1935. $40

8
TARZAN Whitman Better Little Book #1444 © 1945. $40

9
TARZAN 4x4″ ''Tarzan Ice Cream Cup Lids'' premium booklet by Whitman © 1935. $100

10
TARZAN 3.5x4″ Whitman booklet © 1938. $100

11
TARZAN 3.5x6″ Whitman booklet © 1935. $100

12
TARZAN TWINS 3.5x6″ Whitman booklet © 1935. $100

13
TARZAN 3x7″ bwr cardboard advertising bookmark by Grosset & Dunlap. 1930s. $40

14
TARZAN 7.5x9.5″ Whitman Big Big Book © 1936. $75

15
TARZAN 10.5x15.5″ Saalfield coloring book © 1933. $250

16
TARZAN 8x9″ ''Pop-Up'' book by Blue Ribbon Press © 1935. $200

17
TARZAN 7.5x10″ comic strip book © 1940. $250

18
TARZAN 5.5x8″ Whitman book © 1954. $15

19
ELMO LINCOLN AUTOGRAPH on 6.5x8.5″ bw photo with signature date 1919. $100

20
ELMO LINCOLN 1x2.5″ English tobacco premium card c. 1920s. $20

21
ELMO LINCOLN 8x9″ diecut paper mask undated but for 1921 film title. $275

22
''SON OF TARZAN'' 3x6″ cardboard ink blotter ad for silent film serial c. mid-1920s. $100

23
TARZAN & ANIMALS 7x9″ paper masks including those of Akut The Ape and Numa The Lion.
1933.   TARZAN $75, ANIMALS EACH $25

24
''FAMILY CIRCLE'' 8.5x11″ magazine issue for May 25, 1934 with Tarzan/Weissmuller cover article. $25

25
''TARZAN ESCAPES'' 6x8″ Wheaties box back panel for undated but 1936 Weissmuller film. $50

26
''TIP TOP COMICS'' 11x14″ ad card picturing issue #18 published for October 1937. $200

13

14

15

16

17

18

19

20

21

22

23

24

25

26

27

28

29

30

31   **32**

33

34

35

36

27
TARZAN 3x6x10″ boxed "Electric Target Game" with battery operated target. 1930s. BOXED $200, TARGET ONLY $125

28
"TARZAN TREASURE LAND" 1x7x7″ long boxed solitaire tile game © 1934. $250

29
"SIGNAL TARZAN CLUB" 1″ yellow/green/black celluloid premium button by Signal Oil Co. 1930s. $75

30
TARZAN 2.5x3″ card from strip card set © 1936. EACH $25

31
TARZAN 1.25x2.5″ card from English set of 50 by Ogden's Cigarettes c. 1936. $20

32
TARZAN 1.25x2.5″ card from English movie star set c. 1935. $20

33
TARZAN 2.5x3.5″ cards from English set of 66 by Anglo Confectionary Ltd. © 1966. EACH $1

34
TARZAN 14x20″ "Jungle Map And Treasure Hunt" premium game sheet from Weston's Biscuits of England in 7.5x10″ envelope. © 1933.
COMPLETE $350, NO ENVELOPE $250

35
TARZAN 5″ tall or shorter hollow plaster premium figures by Fould's Macaroni for painting by recipient. c. 1934. PEOPLE EACH $35, ANIMALS EACH $15

36
"TARZAN CASEIN GLUE" 2.5″ diameter by 4″ tall product canister. 1930s. $75

37
''TARZAN ICE CREAM CUP''
9.5x19″ full color poster.
1930s. $300

38
''TARZAN CUPS'' 11x17″ full color
poster. 1930s. $250

39
''TARZAN CUPS'' 5x18″ full color
poster. 1930s. $150

40
''TARZAN'S NEW YORK ADVEN-
TURE'' 27x41″ one-sheet re-issue
poster for original 1942 movie
c. 1950s. $90

41
''TARZAN FINDS A SON'' 11x16″
four-page publicity herald for movie
of 1939. $150

42
''TARZAN AND THE SHE-DEVIL''
12x18″ pressbook for movie of
1953. $50

43
''TARZAN'S GREATEST JUNGLE
ADVENTURE'' 12x12″ album of
three 78 rpm records by Tarzan Studios, Hollywood. 1940s. $90

44
''TARZAN SONG'' 7x7″ envelope
with Golden Record © 1952. $15

45
''TARZAN'' 6″ diameter full color
celluloid button © 1974. $30

46
''TARZAN, LORD OF THE JUN-
GLE'' 8x10″ full color animation cel
for TV series by Filmation
c. 1980s. $125

37

38

39

40

41

42

43

44

45

46

Terry and the Pirates

Creator: Milton Caniff

Began: (D) 10/22/34; (S) 12/9/34. Chicago Tribune-New York News Syndicate.

Later Artists and/or Writers: George Wunder.

Principal Characters: Terry, Pat Ryan, Connie, Dragon Lady, April Kane, Burma, (later) Col. Flip Corkin, Hotshot Charlie.

Synopsis: Adventure strip combining Oriental, exotic and suspense story elements including numerous encounters with Asian evil-doers. The strip was continued by George Wunder after Caniff's departure in 1946 to begin the Steve Canyon strip early the following year. The strip ceased in 1973.

1

2

3

4

5

6

7

8

9

10

11

12

1
TERRY 7.5x9.5" Whitman Big Big Book #4073 © 1938. $125

2
TERRY Whitman Better Little Book #1492 © 1944. $35

3
TERRY Whitman Better Little Book #1420 © 1946. $35

4
TERRY 2.5x2.75" Whitman Penny Book © 1938. $15

5
TERRY 3.5x3.5" Tarzan Cup premium booklet © 1936. $75

6
TERRY 4x5.5" Dell Fast-Action book c. 1940s. $75

7
TERRY 8x9.5" "Pop-Up" book by Blue Ribbon Press © 1935. $175

8
TERRY 8x11" Saalfield coloring book © 1946. $25

9
TERRY 8.5x11" Saalfield coloring book © 1946. $35

10
TERRY Large Feature comic book #6 © 1936. $230

11
TERRY "APRIL KANE" 5.5x8" Whitman book with dust jacket © 1942. $25

12
TERRY 7x10" Random House book © 1946. $35

13
TERRY 2x9x17″ wide boxed Whitman game © 1937. $75

14
"TERRYSCOPE" 1.5x1.5x9″ long assembled cardboard periscope from diecut parts offered as Libby Food premium © 1941. $350

15
TERRY "TREASURE HUNTER'S GUIDE" 3.5x6″ premium booklet by Dari-Rich Chocolate Drink © 1938. $15

16
TERRY 7.5x10″ rwb cardboard "Victory Airplane Spotter" disk wheel with envelope. Libby Foods premium © 1942. $150

17
TERRY 7x10.5″ paperdoll and activity book by Libby Foods © 1941. $125

18
TERRY 5x7″ envelope holding pair of "Tattoo Transfers" premium sheets by Coco-Wheats c. early 1940s. $75

19
TERRY "HINGEES" 7.5x11″ envelope pack of punch-out character figures for assembly. 1940s. $75

20
TERRY CHARACTER 2.75x2.75″ waxed paper bread loaf end labels from series of 1940s. EACH $15

21
TERRY 3.5x7.5″ premium comic booklet by Canada Dry © 1953. $40

22
TERRY 2x12x15.5″ tall boxed "Sunday Funnies" game by Ideal © 1972. $30

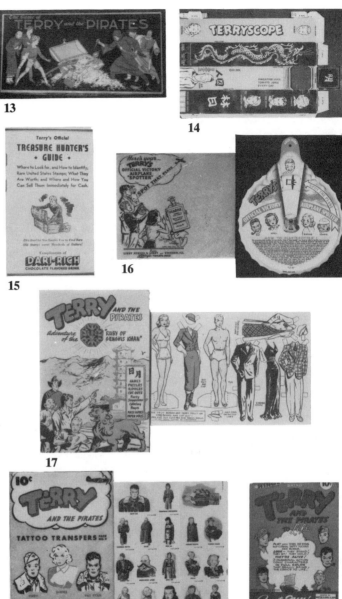

Tillie the Toiler

Creator: Russ Westover

Began: (D) 1/3/21; (S) 10/8/22. King Features Syndicate.

Later Artists and/or Writers: Bob Gustafson.

Principal Characters: Tillie Jones, faithful suitor Mac (Clarence MacDougall), her boss Mr. Simpkins, supervisor Wally Whipple.

Synopsis: Strip based around an attractive girl working in a fashion salon, noted for wearing trendy fashion clothing researched by Westover. Stories were frequently spiced by her romantic encounters, inevitably ending by her return to co-worker Mac. A 1927 movie starred Marion Davies in the title role. The strip ceased in 1959.

1

2

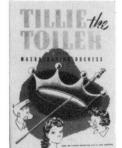

3

4

5

6

7

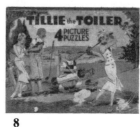

8

1
TILLIE 10x10″ Cupples & Leon book © 1925. $40

2
TILLIE 10.5x13″ Whitman paperdoll book © 1942. $125

3
TILLIE 5.5x8″ Whitman book with dust jacket © 1943. $15

4
TILLIE 9x12″ coloring book by Gabriel c. 1930s. $35

5
TILLIE ORIGINAL ART on 5.5x22.5″ white cardboard inked in black by Russ Westover for daily newspaper strip of April 7, 1934. $125

6
TILLIE AND MAC four 7.25x9.75″ full color sample notebook covers © 1928. EACH $15

7
TILLIE 8x10″ full color jigsaw puzzle issued as newspaper supplement © 1933. $12

8
TILLIE 2x8x10″ wide boxed set of four full color jigsaw puzzles © 1933. $50

Tom Corbett, Space Cadet

Creator: Paul Newman (writer), Ray Bailey (artist)

Began: (S) 9/9/51. Field Newspaper Syndicate.

Principal Characters: Space Cadets Tom Corbett, Roger Manning, T. J. Thistle, Astro, Captain Strong.

Synopsis: Spinoff comic strip from the popular early 1950s television series set during the 24th century at the Space Academy for Training of Solar Guards. Newspaper publication ceased in September 1953.

1
TOM CORBETT 5.5x7.5″ Book No. 1 with dust jacket. From set of eight published by Grosset & Dunlap © 1952. $12

2
TOM CORBETT Book No. 2 from same set as #1 © 1953. $12

3
TOM CORBETT Book No. 3 from same set as #1 © 1953. $12

4
TOM CORBETT Book No. 4 from same set as #1 © 1953. $15

5
TOM CORBETT Book No. 5 from same set as #1 © 1954. $15

6
TOM CORBETT Book No. 6 from same set as #1 © 1954. $15

7
TOM CORBETT Book No. 7 from same set as #1 © 1955. $15

8
TOM CORBETT Book No. 8 from same set as #1 © 1956. $15

9
TOM CORBETT 6.5x8″ Wonder Book © 1953. $12

10
TOM CORBETT 11x15″ Saalfield coloring book © 1952. $30

11
TOM CORBETT 11x15″ Saalfield coloring book © 1953. $40

12
TOM CORBETT 8x11″ Saalfield coloring book c. 1952. $40

13

14

15

16

17

18

19

20

21

22

23

24

25

26

27

13
TOM CORBETT 8x11″ Saalfield coloring book © 1953. $40

14
TOM CORBETT 7x10″ Prize Publications Vol. 2 #3 comic book
© 1955. $60

15
TOM CORBETT 7x10″ Dell Comic #421 c. 1954. $35

16
TOM CORBETT 10x14″ punch-out book c. 1953. $60

17
TOM CORBETT 7.5x8″ Album 1 for 24 bread loaf labels © 1952. $75

18
TOM CORBETT 10x11″ boxed Saalfield set of three jigsaw puzzles
© 1952. $75

19
TOM CORBETT 12x16″ Saalfield tray puzzle © 1952. $40

20
TOM CORBETT 3″ tall plastic ''Rocket-Lite'' pin and 2.25x3.75″ related membership card c. 1952.   PIN $60, CARD $20

21
TOM CORBETT 3.5x5.5″ bw photo c. 1952. $30

22
TOM CORBETT 5x7″ bwr club member certificate c. 1952. $40

23
''SPACE CADET'' 2x4″ Kellogg premium fabric patch c. 1952. $40

24
TOM CORBETT 3x4″ vinyl wallet edged in brass. Early 1950s. $50

25
CORBETT 4.5x4.5″ set of three View-Master reels with booklet
© 1954. $30

26
CORBETT identical to #25 but with revised envelope and booklet.
c. 1954. $40

27
''SPACE CADET'' 7″ long metal flashlight. Early 1950s. $50

28
TOM CORBETT "SPACE ACADEMY" 4x14x22" wide boxed Marx playset #7012. Early 1950s. COMPLETE $600

29
TOM CORBETT 2x11x16" wide boxed figure mold and coloring set. Early 1950s. $100

30
TOM CORBETT 7x7x7" Philco TV premium paper mask picturing him plus Howdy Doody characters and Gabby Hayes on remaining three panels. c. 1952. $125

31
TOM CORBETT 6x12x14" tall box holding plastic assembly parts for "Cosmic Vision" helmet. Early 1950s. $125

32
TOM CORBETT 6x9" card holding balloon launching toy by Oak Rubber Co. Early 1950s. $40

33
TOM CORBETT 10" long full color tin space pistol in box by Marx. Early 1950s. BOXED $150, LOOSE $100

34
TOM CORBETT 24" long plastic clicker rifle with box by Marx. Early 1950s. BOXED $175, LOOSE $125

35
TOM CORBETT 4.5x5" black metal binoculars with box c. 1952. BOXED $100, LOOSE $75

36
TOM CORBETT wristwatch with original straps. By Ingraham c. 1951. $90

37
TOM CORBETT 6x6" envelope holding 78 rpm record of Space Academy Song and Space Cadet March. Early 1950s. $25

38
TOM CORBETT 2.5x3.5" black leather belt buckle with small metal rocketship. Early 1950s. $40

28

29

30

31

32

33

34

35

36

37

38

Toonerville Folks

Creator: Fontaine Fox

Began: 1908 (weekly) Chicago Post; (D) 1913, (S) 1918. Wheeler Syndicate. Later Bell and McNaught Syndicates.

Principal Characters: Mickey (Himself) McGuire, Skipper and his Trolley, Powerful Katrinka, Aunt Eppy Hogg, Terrible-Tempered Mr. Bang, Snake-Tongue Tompkins, Grandma Demon Chaperone, Uncle Chew Wilson, Pinckney Wortle, Little Woo-Woo Wortle.

Synopsis: Semi-rural comedy strip about the Toonerville community, its extensive cast of eccentric residents, and its famous Trolley, a rather hapless vehicle but still the town's only claim to fame. The strip ceased in 1955.

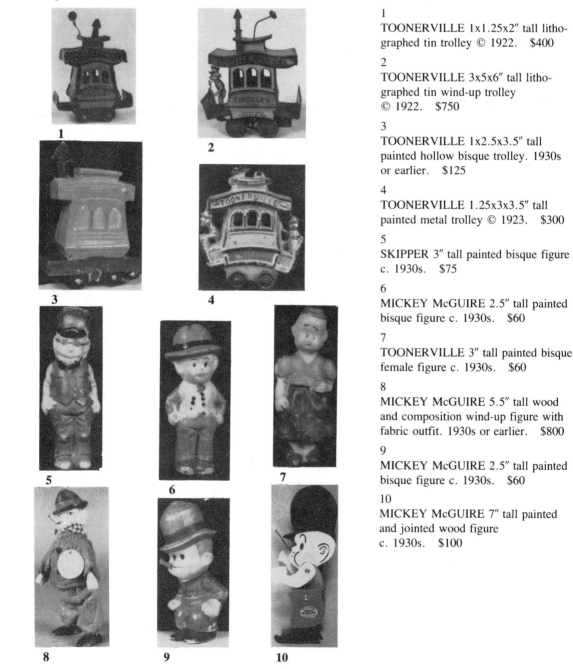

1
TOONERVILLE 1x1.25x2″ tall lithographed tin trolley © 1922. $400

2
TOONERVILLE 3x5x6″ tall lithographed tin wind-up trolley
© 1922. $750

3
TOONERVILLE 1x2.5x3.5″ tall painted hollow bisque trolley. 1930s or earlier. $125

4
TOONERVILLE 1.25x3x3.5″ tall painted metal trolley © 1923. $300

5
SKIPPER 3″ tall painted bisque figure c. 1930s. $75

6
MICKEY McGUIRE 2.5″ tall painted bisque figure c. 1930s. $60

7
TOONERVILLE 3″ tall painted bisque female figure c. 1930s. $60

8
MICKEY McGUIRE 5.5″ tall wood and composition wind-up figure with fabric outfit. 1930s or earlier. $800

9
MICKEY McGUIRE 2.5″ tall painted bisque figure c. 1930s. $60

10
MICKEY McGUIRE 7″ tall painted and jointed wood figure c. 1930s. $100

11
TOONERVILLE 8x10.5" book published by Doran Co. © 1917. $175

12
TOONERVILLE 10x10" Cupples &
Leon book © 1921. $75

13
"TOONERVILLE FOLKS"
2x3x5.25" wide full color box for
"Uneeda" crackers c. 1930. $150

14
"TOONERVILLE TROLLEY"
1.5x8x16" wide boxed Milton Bradley
game c. 1930s. $125

15
"TOONERVILLE FOLKS" ORIGI-
NAL ART on 11x13.5" white sheet
inked in black by Fontaine Fox
c. 1930s. $200

16
"TOONERVILLE TOWN" 10x17"
cardboard sheet of full color cut-outs.
Premium by Vaseline Petroleum Jelly
c. 1930s. $150

17
TOONERVILLE 3.5x6.25" full color
advertising folder for Coca-Cola
© 1931. $50

18
TOONERVILLE 3.5x6.25" advertising folder for Coca-Cola. Photo shows
cover plus sample pages.
© 1931. $50

11

12

13

14

15

16

17

18

Winnie Winkle

Creator: Martin Branner

Began: (D) 9/20/20; (S) 4/2/22. Chicago Tribune-New York News Syndicate.

Later Artists and/or Writers: Jack Berrill, Max van Bibber, Jean Sparber, Joe Kubert, Frank Bolle.

Principal Characters: Winnie Winkle, brother Perry Winkle, Ma and Rip Winkle, Mr. Bibbs, Denny Dimwit, Will Wright.

Synopsis: Originally titled *Winnie Winkle The Breadwinner*, the strip is one of the earliest to depict the working female in serious vein. The strip in early form also included the antics of her younger adolescent brother, Perry, and his cohorts known as The Rinkydinks. Winnie was married in 1937 to Will Wright who shortly thereafter was dropped from the strip and Winnie's subsequent life.

1

2

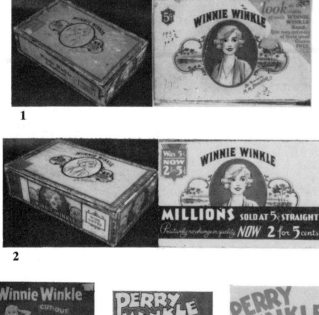

3   **4**   **5**

6   **7**   **8**

1
WINNIE WINKLE 2.5x5.5x9.25″ wide wood cigar box with full color inside lid label c. 1930s. $30

2
WINNIE WINKLE 2.5x5.5x9.25″ wide wood cigar box with full color inside lid label c. 1930s. $30

3
WINNIE WINKLE 8.5x11″ Fun Time cut-out and coloring book c. 1950s. $75

4
PERRY WINKLE Whitman Better Little Book #1487 © 1938. $30

5
PERRY WINKLE Whitman Big Little Book #1199 © 1937. $30

6
WINNIE WINKLE 1x5x7″ tall boxed ''Pillsbury's Comicooky Baking Set'' © 1937. $40

7
PERRY WINKLE 2.5″ tall painted bisque figure with nodder head c. 1930s. $75

8
WINNIE WINKLE 1¼″ blw celluloid newspaper contest button c. 1930s. $20

Wonder Woman

Creator: William Moulton Marston (writer, pen name Charles Moulton), H. G. Peter (artist)

Began: 1944.

Principal Characters: Wonder Woman (alter ego Diana Prince), romantic interest Capt. Steve Trevor.

Synopsis: Very short-lived comic strip based on popularity of comic book heroine created in 1941, although popularity continues to the present in comic book form, plus mid-1970s TV versions. Wonder Woman was the first female superhero to attain mass popularity.

1 ''WONDER WOMAN'' DC Comic #21 for Jan.-Feb. 1947. $165

2 ''WONDER WOMAN'' DC Comic #23 for May-June 1947. $165

3 ''WONDER WOMAN'' 8x10.5'' English annual book for 1980. $20

4 ''WONDER WOMAN''   3½'' full color celluloid button #14 from ''Super Hero Club'' series © 1966. $15

5 ''WONDER WOMAN'' 1.5x8.5x16.5'' wide boxed Hasbro game © 1967. $35

6 WONDER WOMAN 8'' tall plastic action figure with fabric outfit by Mego © 1972. $35

7 WONDER WOMAN 4'' tall Pez candy dispenser variations with hard plastic or soft vinyl head, both c. 1970s. SOFT HEAD $35, HARD (RED HAIR) $75, HARD (BLACK HAIR) $3

8 ''WONDER WOMAN'' 6.5'' tall glass tumbler premium from Pepsi Super Series © 1976. $12

9 ''WONDER WOMAN'' 11'' tall vinyl hand puppet by Ideal © 1966. $20

10 ''WONDER WOMAN'' 4.5'' diameter by 7'' tall painted composition music box © 1978. $35

11 WONDER WOMAN 6'' tall ''Super Junior'' vinyl squeaker figure © 1978. $25

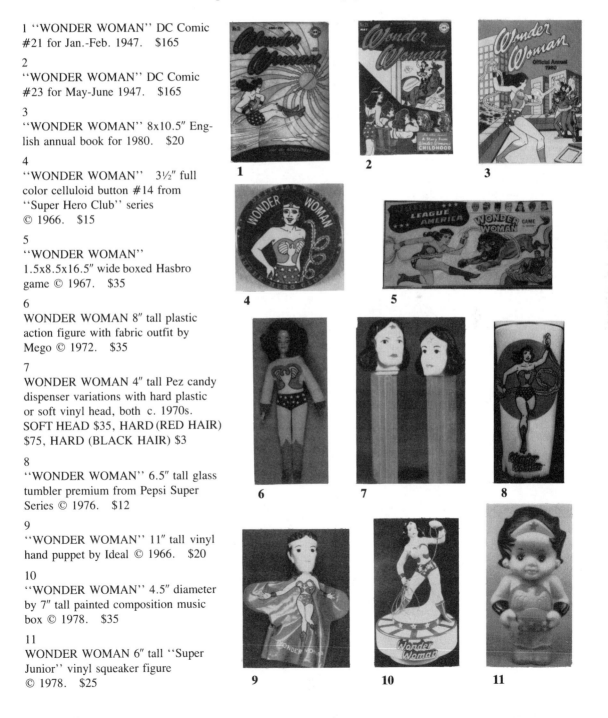

1   2   3

4   5

6   7   8

9   10   11

The Yellow Kid

Creator: Richard F. Outcault

Began: 5/5/1895 New York World; 1896 Hearst Syndicate.

Later Artists and/or Writers: George Luks.

Principal Character: The Yellow Kid.

Synopsis: The earliest and also one of the most remembered newspaper comic strips, centered around a bald, homely waif clad in a nightshirt inscribed with his comments and opinions. The Yellow Kid appeared first in a panel titled *At The Circus in Hogan's Alley*. The Yellow Kid title began in 1896 with a syndication change to Hearst Newspapers. Outcault dropped the character in 1898 to move on to another, Poor Li'l Mose, and eventually to Buster Brown.

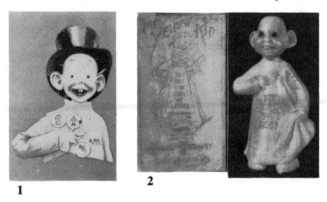

1

3

4

5

1
YELLOW KID 8.5x11.5″ full color portrait cut from larger High Admiral Cigarettes paper sign c. 1896. $200

2
YELLOW KID 4″ tall soap figure in 2x2.5x4.25″ tall box c. 1896.
BOXED $400, LOOSE $200

3
YELLOW KID 3x4.5″ jigsawed wood head that probably originally held calendar on the chest. c. 1896. $150

4
YELLOW KID 8″ tall fabric hand puppet with composition head c. 1896. $400

5
YELLOW KID 3.5″ tall metal figure missing stuffed fabric pin cushion from side. c. 1896. $300

6
YELLOW KID 4.75″ tall metal chocolate mold c. early 1900s. $300

7
YELLOW KID 7″ tall white metal statue c. 1896. $300

6

7

8
YELLOW KID 1x1.5x1.5″ tall cast
iron cap bomb with mouth that opens
for placement of cap. c. 1896. $200

9
"THE YELLOW KID" 7x9″ Vol. 1
#2 issue of biweekly magazine for
April 3, 1897. $300

10
"THE YELLOW KID" 7x9″ Vol. 1
#3 issue of biweekly magazine for
April 17, 1897. $300

11
"NEW YORK JOURNAL'S COL-
ORED SUNDAY SUPPLEMENT"
18x24″ full color paper poster including Yellow Kid art and "Hogan's Alley" illustrations by R. F. Outcault.
Poster is for forthcoming October 18
Sunday edition which documents to
1896. $2000

12
NEW YORK "SUNDAY WORLD"
12x18″ full color poster with Yellow
Kid art by George Luks. Poster is for
forthcoming November 1 edition that
documents to 1896. $400

13
"TECHNIQUE" MAGAZINE 10x20″
yellow/bw paper poster with probable
art by George Luks for forthcoming
April 22, 1898 issue. $400

14
YELLOW KID 10x17″ full color single panel cartoon from New York
World edition for Sunday, May 17,
1896. $150

15
YELLOW KID 18x22″ full color single panel cartoon from New York
World edition for Sunday, September
6, 1896. $200

8

9

10

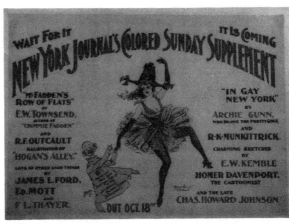

11

12

13

14

15

16

18

17

19

20

21

22

23

24

25

26

27

28

16
YELLOW KID 7x8.5″ school composition book © 1896 by Outcault. $250

17
YELLOW KID 8.25x10.5″ sheet music folder from newspaper. Photo shows front and back. © 1896. $250

18
YELLOW KID 2.5x6.25″ diecut thin cardboard bookmark premium by candy company c. 1896. $75

19
YELLOW KID 3x5″ advertising card for Fleischmann's Yeast c. 1896. $100

20
YELLOW KID 6.5″ tall diecut full color advertising card for Elk Baking Powder c. 1896. $125

21
YELLOW KID 3x4.5″ card #15 from set of 25 by Adams Chewing Gum © 1896.   EACH $25

22
YELLOW KID card set similar to #21 except for colors.   EACH $25

23
YELLOW KID 3.5x5.5″ full color monthly advertising card for September 1912. $40

24
SAME AS #23 except for October 1912. $40

25
SAME AS #23 except for March 1913. $40

26
SAME AS #23 except for April 1913. $40

27
SAME AS #23 except for January 1914. $40

28
SAME AS #23 except for February 1914. $40

29
YELLOW KID 1x4x4″ metal printer's plate on wood block for product ad dated 1910. $125

30
SAME AS #29 except for product ad. $125

31
SAME AS #29 except for product ad. $125

32
SAME AS #29 except for product ad. $125

33
SAME AS #29 except for product ad. $125

34
SAME AS #29 except for product ad. $125

35
YELLOW KID 4x5.25x9.5″ wide wood cigar box. Photo shows top and underside of lid. © 1896. $400

36
YELLOW KID 3.5x5.5x9″ wide wood cigar box version with engraved lid art. c. 1896. $400

37
YELLOW KID 1¼″ colorful celluloid pin-back button #18 from numbered series 1-94 by High Admiral Cigarettes picturing him with various sayings. c. 1896. #1-40 EACH $25, #41-89 EACH $50, #90-94 EACH $100

38
YELLOW KID 1¼″ colorful celluloid pin-back button similar to #37 but from series numbered 101-160 showing him with flags, mostly of various countries. c. 1896. EACH $40

29   **30**

31   **32**

33   **34**

35

36

37   **38**

Yogi Bear

Creator: Hanna-Barbera Studios.

Began: 1958 (ABC-TV), McNaught Syndicate 1961.

Principal Characters: Yogi Bear, girlfriend Cindy Bear, youngster Boo Boo Bear, Ranger Smith, bulldog Chopper, duckling Yakky Doodle, tiger Snagglepuss, Fibber Fox, Alfy Gator.

Synopsis: First introduced on the Hanna-Barbera late 1950s animated *Huckleberry Hound Show,* Yogi remains popular to present day as the brazen ("smarter than the average bear"), wily, and ever-hungry procurer of picnic eatables at Jellystone National Park. His cunning methods of pilfering picnic baskets continually befuddle tourists as well as the constantly-outwitted Ranger Smith.

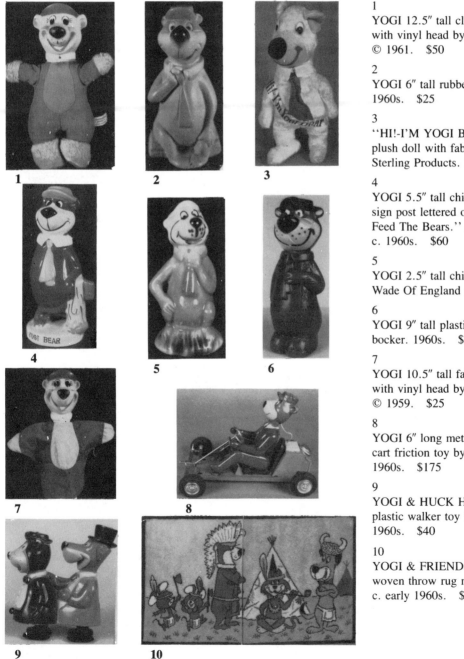

1
YOGI 12.5″ tall cloth and plush doll with vinyl head by Knickerbocker © 1961. $50

2
YOGI 6″ tall rubber squeeze toy. 1960s. $25

3
"HI!-I'M YOGI BEAR" 16″ tall plush doll with fabric name sash by Sterling Products. 1960s. $50

4
YOGI 5.5″ tall china figurine with sign post lettered on reverse "Don't Feed The Bears." Japanese c. 1960s. $60

5
YOGI 2.5″ tall china figurine by Wade Of England c. 1960. $125

6
YOGI 9″ tall plastic bank by Knickerbocker. 1960s. $35

7
YOGI 10.5″ tall fabric hand puppet with vinyl head by Knickerbocker © 1959. $25

8
YOGI 6″ long metal and plastic go-cart friction toy by Linemar. 1960s. $175

9
YOGI & HUCK HOUND 3.5″ tall plastic walker toy by Marx. 1960s. $40

10
YOGI & FRIENDS 22x36″ colorful woven throw rug made in Belgium c. early 1960s. $150

11
YOGI ORIGINAL ART on 21x26″
white cardboard inked in black by
Hanna-Barbera artist for Sunday
newspaper comic strip with art date of
June 24, 1963. $150

12
YOGI ORIGINAL ART on
11.5x13.5″ white cardboard inked in
black by Hanna-Barbera artist for
daily single panel cartoon.
1960s. $50

13
YOGI ORIGINAL ART on
11.5x13.5″ white cardboard inked in
black by Hanna-Barbera artist for
daily single panel cartoon.
1960s. $50

14
YOGI 12x12″ album holding single
"Original TV Soundtracks" 33 1/3
rpm record. 1960s. $15

15
YOGI 4x12x20″ tall boxed "Ball
Toss" target game. Photo shows lid
and target. © 1960. $75

16
"YOGI BEAR'S CIRCUS" 1x5x9″
tall plastic bagatelle marble game by
Marx. 1960s. $40

17
YOGI "GO FLY A KITE" 2x9x17.5″
wide boxed Transogram game. Photo
shows lid plus character playing
pieces. © 1961. $30

18
YOGI 1.5x8x15.5″ wide boxed Milton
Bradley game. Photo shows lid and
playing board. © 1971. $25

11

12   **13**   **14**

15   **16**

17

18

Multi-Character Items

From the earliest years of comic strips to the present, many merchandise or product premium items have been devised to include characters from two or more separate strips. The approach was obviously to broaden the appeal of the particular item. Multi-character collectibles were frequently issued by toy and puzzle makers, book publishers, as well as newspaper syndicates.

1
2
3
4
5
6
7

1
"NORTH AMERICAN'S FUNNY FAMILY" 8x11″ full color calendar sheet newspaper supplement from Sunday, Jan. 2, 1921. $200

2
"KING FEATURES SYNDICATE" 14x22″ full color comic character calendar for 1928 with moveable wheel picturing various characters. $400

3
"ALL THE FUNNY FOLKS" 9.5x12″ book by World Today with full color 112-page story merging characters from 48 different comic strips. Photo shows front cover and example page art. © 1926. $175

4
SAME AS #3 but with dust jacket, pictured in photo. © 1926. $250

5
"YOUR FAVORITE COMIC CHARACTER" 2x2.5x6″ wide rwb box only for composition wood figures c. 1944.   BOX ONLY $50

6
COMIC CHARACTERS 13x16.5″ cloth sheet with full color printed panels of nine King Features Syndicate characters. 1930s. $250

7
"CARTOON CHARACTER" 2x4.5x6.5″ wide boxed set of eight glass Christmas tree lightbulbs. 1930s.   BOXED SET $400, EACH BULB $40

8
"PARAMOUNT CARTOON COM-
ICS" 2x6x12.5" wide boxed set of
eight glass Christmas tree light character bulbs. Photo example has two
replacement bulbs. 1930s.   BOXED
SET $400, EACH BULB $40

9
"FUNNIES FROM FUNNYLAND"
8x10.5" Whitman tablet of 32 illustrated writing sheets plus envelopes
and character gummed seals for characters pictured on cover.
© 1932. $60

10
"KING FEATURES SYNDICATE"
5" tall silvered metal figure titled
"Polar Lark" comprised of faces or
heads of seven characters of that syndicate. © 1926. $350

11
"THE COMIC CLUB" 7x9.5" block
sheet of 19 full color perforated character stamps with gummed backs.
Wrigley Gum premium that also offers
other comic premiums with offer expi-
ration date July 1, 1934. $100

12
"COMIC CLUB MONEY" 2.75x6"
toy currency bills with colorful different character images on front and
back. Photo shows two examples from
series. 1930s.   EACH $10

13
"SEARS TOYLAND" 10.5x13" diecut full color premium comic book
with 12 pages of comic strip reprints
for 14 characters. c. 1939. $130

14
DELL COMIC CHARACTERS 8x10"
full color composite portrait card from
comic book publisher. 1950s. $100

8

9

10

11

12

13

14

15

16

17

18

19

15
''PUCK COMIC WEEKLY/SUNDAY COMICS'' set of eight 13x20'' full color Christmas gift promotion signs c. 1951.   EACH $50

16
KING FEATURES SYNDICATE ''POPULAR COMICS'' 1.5x6x7'' tall boxed set of 16 full color different character Christmas cards with envelopes c. late 1940s-early 1950s. BOXED SET $125, EACH CARD $7

17
FAMOUS ARTISTS SYNDICATE ''POPULAR FUNNIES'' 1.5x5.5x7'' tall boxed set of 16 full color different character birthday or get-well cards with envelopes c. late 1940s-early 1950s.   BOXED SET $125, EACH CARD $7

18
''PICTURE MARBLES'' 1.5x1.5x4.5'' wide boxed set of five colorful glass marbles picturing Betty Boop, Bimbo, Orphan Annie, Skeezix, Moon Mullins. By Peltier Glass Co. c. 1930s.   BOXED SET $400, EACH MARBLE $60

19
KING FEATURES SYNDICATE ''CHRISTMAS GREETINGS'' 1.5x8x10.5'' wide box holding set of 12 silvered plastic 2.5'' tall bell-shaped Christmas ornaments, each with full color decal of different comic character of that syndicate. Pictured are character(s) from Steve Canyon, Beetle Bailey, Little Iodine, Henry, Rip Kirby, Flash Gordon, Prince Valiant, Bringing Up Father, Blondie, Popeye, Snuffy Smith, Buz Sawyer. c. 1950s.   BOXED SET $350, EACH ORNAMENT $25

20
KING FEATURES SYNDICATE
"SING WITH KING AT CHRIST-
MAS" 8x11" folio of Christmas car-
oles with 16 pages illustrated by a like
number of syndicate character singers
plus a double page of Disney characters. © 1949. $60

21
KING FEATURES SYNDICATE 3.5"
diameter by 4" tall cardboard pencil
holder with full color image of nearly
20 characters. Images around upper
perimeter are lightly embossed.
© 1958. $40

22
KING FEATURES SYNDICATE 5x8"
clear glass ashtray with depiction of
14 syndicate characters in red/blue/
black/fleshtone. c. 1950s. $50

23
KING FEATURES SYNDICATE
"ALL STAR COMICS" 1x5x7" wide
boxed card game with full color playing cards from about 10 different
comic strips. © 1934. $75

24
"KOMIC KAMERA" 2x2.5x5" wide
boxed tin film viewer with original
single filmstrip featuring one of pictured characters on box lid. Both lid
and viewer have full color images. By
Allied Mfg. Co. © 1934.   BOXED
$125, LOOSE $75

20

21

22

23

24

25

26

27

28

29

30

31

32

33

25
"FAMOUS KOMICS IN MOVIE STYLE" 2x5x7" wide boxed set of plastic viewer and original three film-strips featuring characters from those pictured on box lid. 1930s. $125

26
COMIC CHARACTER 5.5x7" German-published mechanical valentine card with full color image of 11 characters, each with movable eyes and jaw. Images include unauthorized versions of Barney Google, Spark Plug, Maggie and Jiffs plus others. c. 1920s. $35

27
"FAVORITE FUNNIES PRINTING SET" 1x12x15" wide boxed stamp blocks and related materials by StamperKraft © 1935. $100

28
"NOXZEMA" 12x18" full color double-sided paper hanger sign for drugstore © 1954. $30

29
"FAVORITE FUNNIES PRINTING SET" 2x6.5x9" wide boxed kit of character stamp blocks and related materials by StamperKraft © 1935. $100

30
"MENTHOLATUM" 12x18" full color double-sided paper hanger sign for drugstore © 1954. $30

31
"FAVORITE FUNNIES PRINTING SET" boxed 1x10x11" wide kit of character stamp blocks and related materials by Superior Co. c. late 1940s. $75

32
"PLAYSTONE FUNNIES KASTING KIT" boxed 2x12.5x15.5" wide set of rubber molds and related materials to form character figures. By Allied Mfg. Co. © 1936. $100

33
"THE CARTOONIST COOKBOOK" 5.5x8.5" recipe book with 184 pages accented by art of 45 cartoonists. By Gramercy Publishing Co. © 1964. $25

APPENDIX

CLUBS AND PUBLICATIONS

The following clubs and publications have requested inclusion in this book. Some have broad interests in comic strip collectibles while others are devoted to specific characters or types of collectibles. Be sure to include a self-addressed, stamped envelope when writing for additional information.

AMERICAN GAME COLLECTORS ASSN. Interests include games, puzzles and related playthings. Publications are *Game Times* and *Game Researchers' Notes*. Annual fall convention, annual dues $25. Contact: Secretary, American Game Collectors Assn., 49 Brooks Ave., Lewiston, ME 04240.

ANTIQUE TOY WORLD. Monthly publication dedicated to all toys. Annual subscription $25. Contact: *Antique Toy World*, PO Box 34509, Chicago, IL 60641. Phone: (312) 725-0633.

COLLECTOR GLASS NEWS. Quarterly publication on fast food, cartoon, sports and promotional glassware. Annual subscription $14 (first class), $10 (bulk rate). Contact: *Collector Glass News*, P.O. Box 308, Slippery Rock, PA 16057. Phone: (412) 946-8126.

COMIC BUYER'S GUIDE. Weekly news publication on comics and creators, comic book reviews, show calendars, comic market. Free sample, annual subscription $33.95. Contact: *Comic Buyer's Guide*, 700 E. State St., Iola, WI 54990. Phone: (715) 445-2214.

DOODYVILLE HISTORICAL SOCIETY. Memorabilia of the Howdy Doody television show and related. Publishes *The Howdy Doody Times*. Annual dues $16. Contact: Jeff Judson, 8 Hunt Court, Flemington, NJ 08822. Phone: (908) 782-1159.

DOUBLE RR-BAR NEWS. Bimonthly newsletter devoted to Roy Rogers and related memorabilia and collectibles. Subscription $12 for six issues. Contact: Judy or Jim Wilson, J&J Productions, 3438 Scioto Trail, Portsmouth, OH 45662. Phone: (614) 354-2222.

FLAKE: THE BREAKFAST NOSTALGIA MAGAZINE. Five times annually publication on cereals and related. Annual subscription $20 including free 25-word classified ad with subscription. Contact: *Flake: The Breakfast Nostalgia Magazine*, P.O. Box 481, Cambridge, MA 02140. Phone: (617) 492-5004.

FRIENDS OF HOPALONG CASSIDY. Club to perpetuate memory of him and William Boyd. Quarterly publication *Hoppy Talk*. Subscription and annual dues $15. Annual convention first Saturday in May. For club information contact: John Spencer, P.O. Box 3674, Frederick, MD 21701. For subscription contact: Laura Bates, 6310 Friendship Dr., New Concord, OH 43762-9708. Phone: (614) 826-4850.

THE INSIDE COLLECTOR. Published nine times annually with color photos plus feature articles on popular antiques and collectibles, show and auction reports, calendar of events. Annual subscription $36. Contact: *The Inside Collector*, 225 Main St., Suite 300, Northport, NY 11768. Phone: 1-800-828-1429 (outside New York State) or (516) 261-8337 (within New York State).

THE MOUSE CLUB. Disneyana, old and new, memorabilia club. Publishes five times annually *The Mouse Club Newsletter* including free want ads and for sale ads. Annual subscription $26. Periodic convention. Contact: Kim or Julie McEwen, 2056 Cirone Way, San Jose, CA 95124. Phone: (408) 377-2590.

NATIONAL FANTASY FAN CLUB (NFFC). Disneyana interest club, monthly publication *Fantasyline* and quarterly publication *The Dispatch*. Subscription to both included in annual dues $20. Contact: *National Fantasy Fan Club*, P.O. Box 19212, Irvine, CA 92713. Phone: (714) 731-4705.

NOVELTY SALT & PEPPER SHAKERS CLUB. Collecting and information sharing group, publishes quarterly newsletter. Annual subscription is included in $20 annual dues (United States, Canada and Mexico) or $25 overseas. Annual convention, usually July. Contact: Irene Thornburg, 581 Joy Rd., Battle Creek, MI 49017. Phone: (616) 963-7954.

THE PAILEONTOLOGISTS RETORT. Bi-monthly publication for lunch box collectors. Annual subscription $30. Contact: *The Paileontologists Retort*, P.O. Box 3255, Burbank, CA 91508. Phone: (818) 846-1342.

PAPER COLLECTORS' MARKETPLACE MAGAZINE. Monthly publication since 1983 for collectors of all types of paper memorabilia. Annual subscription $17.95. Contact: *Paper Collectors' Marketplace Magazine*, P.O. Box 128, Scandinavia, WI 54977-0128. Phone: (715) 467-2379.

PEANUTS COLLECTOR CLUB. Club and quarterly newsletter of same title dedicated to Peanuts comics. Annual subscription to 20-page newsletter $16. National convention every four years. Contact: Andrea Podley, 539 Sudden Valley, Bellingham, WA 98226.

POGO FAN CLUB. Dedicated to Pogo and creator Walt Kelly. Annual October convention, annual dues $5. Publishes bi-monthly *The Fort Mudge Most* including Pogo and Kelly reprints, analysis, collector's information. Annual subscription $20. Contact: Steve Thompson, 6908 Wentworth, Richfield, MN 55423. Phone: (612) 869-6320.

R. F. OUTCAULT SOCIETY. Club devoted to the art of Richard F. Outcault, especially The Yellow Kid, Pore Li'l Mose, Buster Brown. Publishes quarterly *The R. F. Outcault Reader*. Annual subscription $5 includes dues. Contact: Richard Olson, 103 Doubloon Dr., Slidell, LA 70461. Phone: (504) 641-5173.

SPIN AGAIN. Quarterly publication on the world of toys, games and collectibles. Annual subscription $20. Contact: Rick Polizzi, 12210 Nebraska Ave., Los Angeles, CA 90025. Phone: (310) 207-6600. Fax: (310) 207-1330.

TOMART'S ACTION FIGURE DIGEST. Bi-monthly publication devoted to action figure collecting. Annual subscription $25.00. Contact: Tomart Publications, 3300 Encrete Lane, Dayton, OH 45439-1944.

TOY SHOP. Monthly publication on toys and related collectibles. Annual subscription $23.95. Contact: Krause Publications, 700 E. State St., Iola, WI 54990.

TOYS & PRICES. Bi-monthly publication, annual subscription $15.95. Contact: Krause Publications, 700 E. State St., Iola, WI 54990.

THE TV COLLECTOR. Bi-monthly publication for more than 10 years including in-depth articles, interviews, episode guides to past TV series. Annual subscription $17 (United States), $19 (Canada) includes free ads for subscribers. Contact: *The TV Collector*, P.O. Box 1088, Easton, MA 02334. Phone: (508) 238-1179.

WESTERNS & SERIALS. Club and publication dedicated to B-Westerns and serial chapter play movies of the past. Quarterly publication of same title. Annual dues including subscription $16. Contact: Norman Kietzer, Route 1, Box 103, Vernon Center, MN 56090. Phone: (507) 540-3677.

THE WRAPPER. Published eight times annually with ads and articles for non-sport card collectors. Sample copy $2 plus two stamps. Annual subscription $21.25. Contact: *The Wrapper*, 7 Simpson St., Apt. A, Geneva, IL 60134. Phone: (708)208-6511.

BIBLIOGRAPHY

Becker, Stephen. *Comic Art in America*. New York: Simon and Schuster, 1959

Blackbeard, Bill and Martin Williams. eds. *The Smithsonian Collection of Newspaper Comics*. Copublished by Smithsonian Institution Press and Harry N. Abrams, Inc., 1977

Gifford, Denis. *The Great Cartoon Stars: A Who's Who*. London: Jupiter Books, Limited, 1979

Goulart, Ron. ed. *The Encyclopedia of American Comics*. New York: Promised Land Productions, 1990

Hake, Ted. *Hake's Americana & Collectibles Auction Catalogues Nos. 17–120*. York, Pa., 1971–1992

Hake, Ted. *Hake's Guide To TV Collectibles: An Illustrated Price Guide*. Radnor, Pa.: Wallace-Homestead Book Company, 1990

Hake, Ted, and Russ King. *Price Guide To Collectible Pin-Back Buttons 1896–1986*. Reprinted Edition of 1986. Radnor, Pa.: Wallace-Homestead Book Company, 1991

Horn, Maurice. ed. *The World Encyclopedia of Cartoons*. (Second Printing). New York: Chelsea House Publishers, 1980

Horn, Maurice. ed. *The World Encyclopedia of Comics*. (Vol. 1 and Vol. 2). New York: Chelsea House Publishers, 1976

Lesser, Robert. *A Celebration of Comic Art and Memorabilia*. New York: Hawthorn Books, Inc., 1975

O'Sullivan, Judith. *The Great American Comic Strip*. Boston: Bulfinch Press Book. Little, Brown and Company, 1990

Rovin, Jeff. *The Illustrated Encyclopedia of Cartoon Animals*. New York: Prentice Hall Press, 1991

Waugh, Coulton. *The Comics*. New York: The Macmillan Company, 1947

Weist, Jerry. *Original Comic Art: Identification and Price Guide*. New York: Avon Books, 1992.

NAME INDEX

Actual names of persons are listed alphabetically by last name. Names of characters are listed alphabetically by first name. Comic strip titles are listed alphabetically in the Table of Contents.

OTHER COLLECTIBLES PRICE GUIDES
BY
TED HAKE

The Button Book
(out of print)

Buttons in Sets
with Marshall N. Levin

Collectible Pin-Back Buttons 1896–1986: An Illustrated Price Guide
with Russ King

The Encyclopedia of Political Buttons 1896–1972; Political Buttons Book II 1920–1976; Political Buttons Book III 1789–1916

The Encyclopedia of Political Buttons: 1991 Revised Prices for Books I, II, and III

Hake's Guide to Advertising Collectibles 100 Years of Advertising From 100 Famous Companies

Hake's Guide to Presidential Campaign Collectibles: An Illustrated Price Guide to Artifacts from 1789–1988

Hake's Guide to TV Collectibles: An Illustrated Price Guide

Non-Paper Sports Collectibles: An Illustrated Price Guide
with Roger Steckler

Sixgun Heroes: A Price Guide to Movie Cowboy Collectibles
with Robert Cauler

A Treasury of Advertising Collectibles
(out of print)